A
Reformation
Debate

John Calvin
and
Jacopo Sadoleto

Edited by John C. Olin

*With an Appendix
on the Justification
Controversy*

BAKER BOOK HOUSE
Grand Rapids, Michigan 49516

To Marian

who also has patience

Copyright 1966 by John C. Olin

First reprinted 1976 by Baker Book House
with permission of Harper & Row, Publishers

Library of Congress Catalog Card Number: 65-10529

ISBN: 0-8010-2390-4

Ninth printing, September 1991

Printed in the United States of America

Foreword

Why should an exchange of letters more than four centuries ago be of interest to today's busy reader?

Because the writers of these letters focus with uncommon clarity and insight on a highly contemporary question: what is the key to find meaning in our daily existence?

The incidentals of change in culture, the accidentals of change in time and place fall away in the literate wrestling of these two ambassadors to the soul — as much to the soul of twentieth-century post-Christian man as to the soul of the sixteenth-century man poised on the verge of modernity.

Roman Catholic Cardinal Jacopo Sadoleto and Reformer John Calvin are agreed on one fundamental, namely, that Christianity holds the key to the mysteries of man's pilgrimage through time and his destiny thereafter. The two men differ as to the means and the manner of life by which that key can be used to open the door to temporal felicity and eternal beatitude. That difference is instructive for modern men confronted by religious decisions of their own.

Sadoleto pens a shrewdly calculating address to self-interest. More precious to each of us, he says, than any other possession is our immortal soul or everlasting self; more crucial, therefore, than any other decision we can make is that governing our final destiny. Shall one live forever in the presence of God or endure the torments of hell?

For centuries, the Cardinal continues, the Catholic Church has shepherded the humbly obedient through the vicissitudes of time and into the precincts of the heavenly mansions. Led by the Spirit, the Church speaks inviolable and saving truth. Why, then, should men entrust themselves to the novelties of Reform, to the teaching of self-serving renegades from the Church?

The Cardinal's prose reflects the man. It breathes the leisured life of Italian humanism, the urbanity of learning, the caution of the scholar.

Quite different is the language of Calvin — as different as was his intense, involved, harried life from that of Sadoleto. Calvin's is clearly the rhetoric of passion, framed in the knowledge that feeling and will govern behavior. His figures of speech are apt, vivid, though unobtrusive. His words spur to action.

Calvin sounds the keynote of the Reformed understanding of Christianity by immediately discounting self-interest (even self-interest in heaven) as sound motivation. Man is made by God, for God's purposes in history. The Bible is replete with evidence that God's purposes may not accord with man's conceptions of immediate advantage. By obtruding itself between God's will and man's response, self-interest becomes reaction, and leads to repression and stultification. The Cardinal's Church has placed its own interests above those of both God and believer, and stands against reformation and progress.

God wills to rule among men, Calvin continues, by the scepter of His Word. To this scepter the Church must also bow. The Spirit leads the Church only through the Bible, not by special and infallible new revelation. We equally oppose, Calvin says, the Church which claims Spirit-led infallibility and the fanatical sectarians who claim Spirit-given revelations — and we do so by standing firmly on the Word.

Indeed, the Church itself is truly gathered and led only where the Word is faithfully preached. And man's beatitude lies solely in obedience to the dictates of the Scriptures, however costly such obedience may be. The Calvinist saint forgets himself into heaven — and finds when he gets there that even such self-denial has been empowered by the Spirit.

At issue, then and now, is the destiny of the person. Shall we find meaning through Christianity? And if so, by focus on our self-interest or on God's?

For Calvin, it is only by reaching in obedience for what can be grasped and done of the divinely revealed will, here and now, that we may at the same time (by grace) lay hold of citizenship in a Kingdom destined to last forever.

Calvin is obviously stung by the Cardinal's calculating charge that the Reformers were schismatic, for purposes of their own selfish gain. Division in the Church was as abhorrent to Calvin as to Sadoleto. And self-seeking he repudiates by pointing to the material gains, and personal influence, offered the Reformers for returning to Mother Church. The model for us, at risk of comfort and life itself, he says, is the Church of the Apostles. Let an impartial judge decide in this matter, between us and yourselves.

Taking care to answer all of the Cardinal's charges, direct and implied, Calvin writes a reply twice as lengthy as Sadoleto's letter. By so doing, Calvin neatly provides us with a succinct summation of the purposes for which he performed his immense labors and gave his life. Calvin's letter is a kind of charter for the Reformed branch of the Reformation.

His letter is, moreover, one of the few writings in which he permitted himself to transcend the rhetorical plain style he so rigidly imposed on himself elsewhere. The attentive reader will have occasion to perceive, if he carefully studies structure and syntax — even in translation — why scholars conclude that Calvin contributed formative influence to the development of the French language and literature.

Lester DeKoster

Contents

Preface

The Reformation of the sixteenth century was essentially a religious event. Other factors undoubtedly played their part in its coming, course, and manifold consequences, but the event itself, if that term may be used to signify so extended a development, was first and foremost a revolution in the domain of religious faith and practice. It is important, therefore, in the study of the Reformation to give close attention to the religious issues involved, that is, to the doctrines and beliefs that were the subject of controversy and the chief concern of Reformer and Catholic apologist alike. Such, in brief, is the thought underlying this volume. The documents it presents unfold these controversial doctrinal issues, particularly the very basic ones of the authority of Church and Scripture and of the justification of man before God. As formulations of that time, they also give us some of the accent, spirit, and argument in which these issues were discussed. And because of their sources they may be said to bear the mark of high authenticity.

J. C. O.

December 10, 1965

Introduction

I

In March, 1539, Cardinal Jacopo Sadoleto, bishop of Carpentras in southern France, addressed a letter to the magistrates and citizens of Geneva asking them to return to the Catholic faith. The following August, John Calvin replied to Sadoleto, defending the adoption of the Protestant reforms. Both letters are lucid and eloquent statements of their respective positions. The dialogue they embody is polemical, but withal their tone is elevated, and their arguments are substantial. Sadoleto's letter and Calvin's reply constitute one of the most interesting exchanges of Catholic-Protestant views during the Reformation era. Together they afford an excellent introduction to the great religious controversy of the sixteenth century.

But these documents are not statements *in vacuo* of a Catholic and a Protestant position. They were drafted in the midst of the religious conflict that was then dividing Europe. They had their more specific occasion, which in turn had its particular historical background. And they reflect too the temperaments and personal histories of the men who wrote them. Sadoleto's letter has an irenic approach, an emphasis on the unity and peace of the Church highly characteristic of the Christian humanism he represented. Calvin's reply is in part a personal defense, an *apologia pro vita sua*, that records his own religious experience.[1] And its taut, comprehensive

[1] Calvin's two speeches before the judgment seat of God have been understood by his biographers as referring to his own experience and conversion. See John T. McNeill, *The History and Character of Calvinism* (New York, 1954), pp. 116-18; Williston Walker, *John Calvin* (New York, 1906), pp. 73-75; and François Wendel, *Calvin*, tr. Philip Mairet (New York, 1963), pp. 38-39.

argument is characteristic of the disciplined and logical mind of the author of *The Institutes of the Christian Religion.*

This introduction will attempt to provide setting and orientation for reading the two letters. Their intrinsic themes are clearly developed, but the external facts concerning their appearance require a few supplementary words. It may also be useful to point out the relevance of their arguments to the Reformation controversy as a whole. Our presentation then will serve as an introduction to the religious issues raised by the Reformation as well as an account of an important episode in its history. Since the doctrinal issues themselves are historical in point of origin and impact, it is proper that we approach them historically and seek to understand their articulation in the actual context of events.

II

When Jacopo Sadoleto wrote his letter to the Genevans in 1539, he was at the height of his long career and was one of the most eminent and respected members of the Sacred College of Cardinals. Born in Modena in 1477, he had attended the University of Ferrara, where his father was a professor of law.[2] He came to Rome around 1499, continued his classical studies under the patronage of Cardinal Oliviero Caraffa, and rose to prominence in the Roman humanist circle. When Cardinal Giovanni de' Medici became Pope Leo X in 1513, he appointed him a papal secretary, and with this office Sadoleto began his service in the Church. He was made bishop of Carpentras in 1517, but he remained in the Roman Curia throughout the pontificate of Leo X and first visited his diocese in 1523 during the short reign of Adrian VI who did not continue his employ. He returned to Rome early in 1524 to

[2] Richard M. Douglas, *Jacopo Sadoleto, 1477-1547* (Cambridge, Mass., 1959) is a full-scale biography and study of Sadoleto. The present author is deeply indebted to this excellent work.

serve the second Medici pope, Clement VII, as secretary, but he withdrew again to reside in Carpentras just prior to the terrible sack of Rome by mutinous imperial troops in May, 1527.

Carpentras, located in the papal Comtat Venaissin near Avignon, became for Sadoleto a haven from the burdens of an active life and the cares and anxieties of a troubled world. In this tranquil corner of the Provence, he devoted himself to the needs of his people and to the scholarly endeavors of a Christian humanist. Like Erasmus, whose friend he was, he hoped to serve the hard-pressed cause of piety and peace through the learned contributions his retirement would permit him to make.[3] Conscious indeed of the ills and perils of his time, he "saw his role at Carpentras as the defense of good letters and Christian orthodoxy alike."[4]

Sadoleto remained in Carpentras from 1527 to 1536, and during these years he composed some of his most notable works. A humanist dialogue on the education and training of youth, *De liberis recte instituendis,* written in 1530, was the most famous and widely published.[5] An extensive commentary on St. Paul's Epistle to the Romans was the most ambitious and controversial.[6] In this latter work Sadoleto grappled with the question of justification and sought to reconcile the action of divine grace and man's own free will. His overemphasis on man's freedom and his neglect of prevenient grace, however, provoked the censure of both the Sorbonne and Rome in

[3] See Sadoleto's letters to Erasmus of November 20, 1528, and February 12, 1530, in P. S. and H. M. Allen, eds., *Opus epistolarum Erasmi* (12 vols. Oxford, 1906-1958), VII, 534-37, and VIII, 359-61. See also Augustin Renaudet, *Erasme et l'Italie* (Geneva, 1954), pp. 217-18, where Sadoleto is viewed as the model Erasmian Catholic and prelate.

[4] Douglas, p. 73.

[5] Translated by E. T. Campagnac and K. Forbes in *Sadoleto on Education* (Oxford, 1916). See also W. H. Woodward, *Studies in Education during the Age of the Renaissance* (Cambridge, 1924), Ch. IX. The Latin text is in Sadoleto, *Opera quae extant omnia* (4 vols. Verona, 1737-1738), Vol. III.

[6] Douglas, pp. 80-93. The Latin text is in Sadoleto, *Opera,* Vol. IV.

1535, although subsequent clarifications by Sadoleto apparently satisfied his critics. At any rate the theological contretemps that arose did not seriously impair Sadoleto's standing at the papal court. In July, 1536, Pope Paul III, who had succeeded Clement VII two years before, called him back to Rome to assist in the preparation of a reform council.

The Roman interval that followed was marked by Sadoleto's participation on a nine-man commission that convened in November under the presidency of Cardinal Gasparo Contarini to study the question of Church reform.[7] Along with other prelates—Gian Pietro Caraffa, Reginald Pole, Gian Matteo Giberti—who shared many of his views regarding the dire state of affairs in the Church, he collaborated in the drafting of a famous report, the *Consilium de emendanda ecclesia,* which boldly criticized the exaggeration of papal power and called for thoroughgoing ecclesiastical reform.[8] In December Sadoleto, Caraffa, and Pole were raised to the cardinalate.

The *Consilium,* presented to Paul III in March, 1537, is one of the great documents of Catholic reform. It embodies the thought and recommendations of a small though important group, who stressed the urgent need of a reformation *in capite,* if the Protestant challenge was to be met and the Church reunited and restored. As such, it may be viewed as an instrument of reconciliation through reform, consonant with the basic attitude of Sadoleto and inaugurating on his part a sequence of initiatives aimed at ending the religious schism. In June, 1537, he wrote a brief, friendly letter to Luther's colleague, Philip Melanchthon, attempting to open up, though without success, a correspondence with the Wittenberg

[7] Douglas, pp. 101 ff.; Ludwig Pastor, *The History of the Popes from the Close of the Middle Ages,* tr. F. I. Antrobus, R. F. Kerr, *et al.* (40 vols. St. Louis, 1891-1953), XI, 154 ff.

[8] The text of the *Consilium de emendanda ecclesia* is in B. J. Kidd, ed., *Documents Illustrative of the Continental Reformation* (Oxford, 1911), pp. 307-18. See also Pastor, XI, 165-71.

scholar. A year later, in July, 1538, he addressed himself to Johann Sturm, the rector of a new school in Strasbourg, who had recently published the text of the *Consilium* with a critical commentary. As a Catholic reformer speaking to a Protestant moderate, he defended the *Consilium* and himself against Sturm's charges, while professing his friendship for men such as Sturm, Melanchthon, and the Strasbourg Protestant reformer, Martin Bucer. In the summer of 1538 he wrote, although he did not publish, "An Exhortation to the Princes and People of Germany," in which he condemned the Lutheran heresy and rebellion but acknowledged many of the grievances of the German people and affirmed the need for their redress and for the reform of abuses in the Church. "I wish only to exhort men to peace," he wrote Duke George of Saxony.[9]

Sadoleto returned to Carpentras in mid-1538. In May and June he had attended Paul III in Nice at the peace negotiations that the Pope sponsored to end the current hostilities between the Holy Roman Emperor Charles V and Francis I of France.[10] After a truce had been signed, Sadoleto withdrew to his beloved diocese, where he remained until the urgent summons of Paul III brought him back to Rome in 1542 to participate in planning the projected Council of Trent. It was in the early months of this residence at Carpentras that he wrote his letter to the Genevans.

The letter is dated March 18, 1539, and was delivered to the Little Council of Geneva two weeks later by an emissary of Sadoleto, Jean Durand. As an appeal for reunion, the letter is clearly in line with Sadoleto's previous efforts. As an affirmation of the authority and tradition of the Church against the innovations of the Genevan reformers, however, it is

[9] Quoted in Douglas, p. 139. Douglas, Ch. VII discusses the efforts of Sadoleto mentioned above.

[10] These hostilities had erupted in early 1536 and have a bearing on the political struggle in Geneva and on Calvin's arrival there in 1536. On the Nice conference, see Pastor, XI, 283-91.

polemical, resembling the unpublished "Exhortation to the Princes and People of Germany," and has been called, not inappropriately, "the first notable challenge of the Counter-Reformation seeking the recovery of Protestant territory."[11] The particular reason for this "challenge" on the part of Sadoleto lay in the state of affairs that then prevailed in Geneva.

In 1539 that city was at a critical juncture in the course of its Reformation. Protestantism had been established, but in April, 1538, its two prime reformers, Guillaume Farel and John Calvin, had been banished for refusing to abide by certain decisions of the municipal authorities concerning liturgy. The unsettled conditions in the months that followed opened the possibility of a Catholic restoration in the city on Lake Leman. It is in view of this opportunity that Sadoleto made his appeal. The appeal appears to have been solely his idea; it certainly reflects his own thought and approach. There is, however, a plausible tradition that links Sadoleto's letter with a conference of Catholic prelates at Lyons in December, 1538, where the question of a Catholic restoration in Geneva was discussed. According to this version, Sadoleto was commissioned by the Lyons gathering, which included Cardinal Tournon of Lyons and Pierre de la Baume, the ousted bishop of Geneva, to write his letter.[12]

Be that as it may, the letter was occasioned by circumstances in the city. At this time Geneva had only recently won its independence from the Duke of Savoy and the Bishop of Geneva. This political struggle was of long duration, and was comparable to what had occurred in many other medieval towns. In its final phase, however, it involved the introduction

[11] McNeill, p. 154.

[12] Douglas, p. 144, gives credence to this account, and so do the editors of *Ioannis Calvini opera quae supersunt omnia* (59 vols. Brunswick, 1863-1900), V, xliv. A.-L. Herminjard, ed., *Correspondance des réformateurs dans les pays de langue française* (9 vols. Geneva, 1866-1897), V, 266, n. 24, rejects it as unsupported by any evidence; and Emile Doumergue, *Jean Calvin* (7 vols. Lausanne, 1899-1927), II, 678, questions it.

and triumph of Protestantism. As Emile Doumergue points out, "what characterizes the religious Reformation in Geneva is its alliance with political emanicipation."[13]

Prior to the sixteenth century, the government of Geneva was vested in its bishop, who was its lord or *dominus;* in the Duke of Savoy, who controlled the post of *vice-dominus* (or *vidomne*); and in a burgher administration consisting of four elected syndics and three councils—the Little Council, the Council of Sixty, and the General Council.[14] The bishopric, however, after the mid-fifteenth century was little more than an appendage of the house of Savoy, and its incumbents were the creatures and cadets of that princely house. In the early sixteenth century, conflict developed between Duke Charles III of Savoy (1504-1553) and a group of patriotic citizens, led by Philibert Berthelier, who sought to protect and extend the rights of the burgher regime. The Duke smashed the insurgent faction in 1519, but his withdrawal from Geneva in late 1525 because of a troubled situation in Piedmont gave the patriots a new opportunity for action. In 1526 they concluded an alliance with Bern and Freiburg in the Swiss Confederation, and in 1527 they instituted the Council of Two Hundred, which formally assumed the powers of the *vidomne.* The Bishop of Geneva, Pierre de la Baume (1522-1544), acquiesced in this major political change and then fled the city to join the Duke in resisting the patriotic gains. In 1530 the Duke attacked Geneva, but the intervention of Bern and Freiburg saved the city and led in turn to their occupation of the Pays de Vaud as a guarantee that Geneva's new freedom would be respected.

Up to this time Protestantism had barely made its appearance in Geneva, but within the next few years the entry was made and an active and aggressive Protestant movement

---

[13] Doumergue, II, 676.

[14] On the history of Geneva during this period, see Doumergue, II, 97 ff.; Walker, Ch. VII; Kidd, pp. 494 ff.; and Société d'Histoire et d'Archéologie de Genève, *Histoire de Genève des origines à 1798* (Geneva, 1951), pp. 139 ff.

began to develop. One of the chief factors in this was the pressure brought to bear on the Genevan authorities by Bern. Bern, Geneva's ally, had adopted Zwinglian reform in 1528 and was militant in her support of the new faith. She was soon dispatching preachers to neighboring towns and country-side and using her influence to gain a hearing for their doctrines. With her backing Guillaume Farel, a fiery French evangelist, returned to Geneva in December, 1533 (his pre-vious visit to the city in October, 1532, had resulted in his speedy expulsion) and, soon joined by a disciple, Pierre Viret of Orbe, stayed on to lay the foundations of Genevan Prot-estantism. At Bern's insistence a public disputation, with Farel and Viret defending "evangelical truth," was held early in 1534 and a church was subsequently turned over to the reformers. The breach had now been made.

In May, 1534, Freiburg, which remained Catholic, severed her alliance with Geneva, and in July the Bishop, in league with the Duke, launched an unsuccessful attack on the city. The political conflict now merged more distinctly with the religious quarrel. Following the Bishop's defeat the Genevan authorites declared the episcopal see "vacated," and the Protestants, still a minority, became more active in their campaign against Catholic faith and practice. A second public disputation in June, 1535, was a major triumph for the re-formers, after which Farel pressed hard his victory, inspiring an outbreak of image-smashing, gaining the pulpit of the cathedral, and persuading the Council of Two Hundred to suppress the Mass. This latter decision, taken on August 10, 1535, marks Geneva's formal adherence to the Reformation.

If that crucial step had been taken, the city's general security, however, remained more troubled and perilous than ever. Still beleaguered by the Duke of Savoy, she sought new aid from Bern. This aid was forthcoming at a strategic moment in January, 1536, when Bern, taking advantage of the Duke's retreat from Geneva's environs because of a French threat to Savoy (the imminence of war between Francis I and Charles

V over Milan now cast its shadow), declared war on Savoy and proceeded to occupy Geneva and its countryside. Ambitious Bern now attempted to impose her suzerainty on her ally, but Geneva refused to submit and at length secured, in a treaty in August, 1536, Bern's acknowledgment of her independence. Meanwhile, a general assembly of citizens in the cathedral of Geneva on May 21 had ratified the reform measures which the councils had already inaugurated, and had affirmed their will "to live according to the Gospel and the Word of God."[15] The political and religious revolution had been achieved.

It had been achieved, but it had not yet been fully secured and consolidated. The fortunes of war, the resurgence of the Catholic cause, the weakness or failure of Protestant leadership could certainly have reopened the issue and altered the course of these recent events. That such did not occur was due in part at least to the arrival in Geneva of a young French scholar who was a recent convert to Protestantism. In July, 1536, John Calvin, en route to Strasbourg from France, made a long detour through Geneva because of the war that had recently broken out between France and the Emperor. Informed of his presence in the town, Farel entreated and adjured him to remain and help in the task of establishing the reformed Church.[16] Calvin reluctantly gave in, and this accidental though dramatic encounter opened a new phase not only in the history of Geneva and in the life of Calvin, but in the whole progress and course of the Protestant Reformation.

At the time of his arrival in Geneva, Calvin was twenty-seven and stood on the threshold of his great career. He was born July 10, 1509, at Noyon in Picardy.[17] His father, an ecclesiastical notary and solicitor in the service of the Bishop

---

[15] Kidd, pp. 518-19.

[16] Calvin himself tells this story in his autobiographical preface to his *Commentary on the Psalms*, in *Calvin: Commentaries*, tr. J. Haroutunian and L. P. Smith (Vol. XXIII of *The Library of Christian Classics*. London, 1958), p. 53.

[17] On the life of Calvin, see the volumes referred to in n. 1. The most extensive study is to be found in Emile Doumergue's seven monumental volumes.

and cathedral chapter of Noyon, had intended his son for theology. Endowed with a cathedral benefice, the young Calvin was sent to Paris at the age of fourteen to study at the University. He received a Master of Arts degree in 1528 and was then directed by his father to turn from theology to law, which the elder Calvin deemed more lucrative. Accordingly the young scholar journeyed to Orléans and Bourges where he studied with some of the most eminent jurists of his day. But humanist scholarship of a more literary character had captured his attention, and while at Orléans and Bourges he studied Greek with a German Lutheran scholar, Melchior Wolmar. After his father's death in 1531 (his father died ex-communicate because of a quarrel with the cathedral chapter over the closing of an estate), Calvin devoted himself wholly to humanist studies. Back in Paris, he attended the new Collège de France, studied Greek and Hebrew, and in 1532 published his first work, a commentary of Seneca's *De Clementia*.

Classical humanism, however, was not long to remain his chief preoccupation. Sometime in late 1533 or early 1534 he underwent, in his own words, "a sudden conversion" and embraced the doctrines of the Protestant reformers.[18] This great turn in his life has been linked with an address his friend Nicholas Cop, the new rector of the University of Paris, had delivered on All Saints' Day, 1533. The address was thought to be Lutheran in inspiration, and provoked action by the authorities against Cop and others believed to be implicated. Calvin fled Paris and took refuge at Angoulême. There, it appears, he arrived at his decision to break with the old Church and to devote himself to the cause of Protestant reform. He left France late in 1534, because of the stringent measures being taken against heretics, and found haven in Protestant Basel. At Basel he entered into correspondence

[18] *Calvin: Commentaries*, p. 52. Calvin's reply to Sadoleto, as we previously mentioned (n. 1), also throws light on his conversion. See also Wendel, pp. 37-42.

with the Swiss and Strasbourg reformers, and there in March, 1536, he published the first draft of his most famous and important work, *The Institutes of the Christian Religion.*[19] It was soon after this memorable publication that he came to Geneva.

Calvin was first appointed Reader in Holy Scripture in Geneva, but he soon rose to a position of leadership in the Genevan Church alongside the elder Farel. In October he participated with Farel and Viret in a disputation at Lausanne, which led, at the demand of Bern, to the imposition of Protestant reform in that neighboring town. His career as reformer and organizer *par excellence* now began. In January, 1537, he drafted a memorandum on church discipline for the approval of the city councils. This was followed in short order by the publication of a Catechism, based on the *Institutes,* and a Confession of Faith, to which the population, one and all, were to give their adherence.[20] Opposition soon appeared to the discipline and strict uniformity which Calvin sought to impose. In November the General Council refused to enforce the Confession of Faith; subsequently the Council of Two Hundred denied Calvin and Farel the right to excommunicate recalcitrant believers. In the annual election of the four syndics in February, 1538, a magistracy come to office that was hostile to the energetic efforts of Calvin and Farel. A showdown between the reformers and the civil authorities now was imminent.

The affair reached its climax several weeks later. In mid-March the Council of Two Hundred warned Calvin and Farel not to meddle in politics, but to preach the Word of God and abide by the ceremonial practices then sanctioned by Bern, including the use of unleavened bread in the Eucharist and the retention of baptismal fonts.[21] Bern added her own in-

[19] On the editions of the *Institutes,* see Wendel, pp. 111-22.
[20] Kidd, pp. 560-72; Wendel, pp. 50-52.
[21] Kidd, p. 577.

sistence that these ceremonies be observed. Calvin and Farel resisted this dictation, refused to accept the Bernese forms, and on Easter Sunday, in defiance of the order of the magistrates, preached from the pulpits of the two main churches in Geneva, but refused to give Communion. On the following day, April 22, the Council of Two Hundred resolved to establish the ceremonies of Bern and to dismiss Calvin and Farel—an action which the General Council and the Little Council confirmed on April 23, ordering the two reformers to leave the city within three days.[22]

This "revolution of 1538," as Doumergue called it, created a highly unsettled state of affairs and led to further dissension within the reform party.[23] A faction, known as *Guillermins* (after Guillaume Farel), led by a prominent Genevan citizen, Ami Perrin, soon emerged and refused to accept the pastors appointed to succeed the exiles. Schism and collapse now threatened the young Church. Catholics were still numerous in Geneva, and the crisis in the community gave them new hope for the recovery and restoration of the old faith. It was then that Sadoleto, to use the picturesque words of Calvin's future colleague and first biographer, Theodore Beza, "observing his opportunity in the circumstances which had occurred, and thinking that he would easily ensnare the flock, when deprived of its distinguished pastors, under the pretext of neighborhood . . . sent a letter to his, so-styled, most Beloved Senate, Council, and People of Geneva, omitting nothing which might tend to bring them back into the lap of the Romish Harlot."[24]

Sadoleto's letter was written and delivered in March, 1539.

[22] Kidd, pp. 579-80.

[23] Doumergue, II, 676, and 653-713. See also Calvin's two letters of October 1, 1538, and June 25, 1539, to the Church in Geneva, exhorting its members to patience and moderation and respect for their ministers in the crisis that now ensued, in Jules Bonnet ed., *Letters of John Calvin* (4 vols. Philadelphia, 1858), I, 82-88, 142-49.

[24] Beza's *Life of Calvin* in John Calvin, *Tracts and Treatises on the Reformation of the Church,* tr. Henry Beveridge (3 vols. Grand Rapids, Mich., 1958), I, lxxiii.

The Little Council, which had received it, decided that a response should be made, but evidently could find no one capable of making a suitable reply. In May the Genevan magistrates sent the letter to Bern and were notified that the Bernese authorities would sponsor a reply to the Cardinal.[25] Here, too, difficulties developed, and it was not until July 24 that the chief minister, Peter Kuntz, suggested to the Council of Bern that Calvin be asked to respond.[26] This agreed upon, the letter was brought to Calvin, then residing in Strasbourg, by Simon Sulzer, a minister at Bern. Urged by his friends, Calvin in mid-August took up his pen and within six days wrote his reply.[27] It was published, together with Sadoleto's letter, by Wendelin Rihel in Strasbourg early the following month.

III

The two letters speak for themselves, but some comment may be made on the significance of their arguments in terms of the Reformation controversy as a whole. We have already called attention to the fact that the letters reflect the temperament and experience of the two men who wrote them. The Christian humanism of Sadoleto unquestionably informs his epistle; Calvin's own conversion, and the conviction and commitment it inspired, are at the core of his reply. But aside from the personal element in the letters is their relevance to the fundamental issues raised by the Reformation. Here two important points stand out: (1) the question of the Church and its authority and (2) the doctrine of justification by faith alone. These issues are cardinal both for this exchange and for the broader debate of which it is a part.

Sadoleto's letter essentially is a defense of the age-old

25 *I. Calvini opera quae supersunt omnia*, X, 350.
26 Herminjard, V, 372.
27 *Ibid.*

Church against those who would overturn its authority and alter its practices and beliefs. His argument rests on the premise that the Catholic Church is the Church of Christ, "always and everywhere directed by the one Spirit of Christ," erring not, "since the Holy Spirit constantly guides her public and universal decrees and Councils." Through her faith and worship, he maintains, men are saved, submitting in humility and obedience to what she enjoins. Twice he poses the key issue in the most explicit terms: "whether to accord with the whole Church, and faithfully observe her decrees, and laws, and sacraments, or to assent to men seeking dissension and novelty?" And in his conclusion he castigates those who would "tear the spouse of Christ in pieces" and begs the Genevans to return to the unity of faith.

Calvin's reply is lengthier and more diffuse than Sadoleto's appeal, but in essence it rejects this image of the Church—this Catholic concept of the enduring Church of Christ, erring not —in the name of fidelity to the ancient Church and to its touchstone, the Word of God. That Church which Sadoleto exalts Calvin conceives to be corrupt, separated from the Word, "mangled and almost destroyed by the Roman Pontiff and his faction." He accuses Sadoleto of separating the Holy Spirit from the Word, of not recognizing "that the Spirit goes before the Church, to enlighten her in understanding the Word, while the Word itself is like the Lydian stone, by which she tests all doctrines," and he claims that the reformers seek only to restore "that ancient form of the Church," faithful to the scriptural Word. "Ours the Church," he affirms, "whose supreme care it is humbly and religiously to venerate the Word of God, and submit to its authority."

Calvin obviously was not unmindful of the reality of the Church; in one of the most famous parts of his letter he tells how "reverence for the Church" had at first held him back from the new reform doctrines. But he does finally reject the existing Church of Rome, and come to conceive of the au-

thentic Church as that "ancient form" which adheres strictly
to the scriptural Word.[28] This subordination of the Church
to Holy Scripture—and here one must understand that it is
Scripture as grasped and expounded by Calvin and other
reformers—is, without question, the main issue raised by this
exchange. It is the issue of whether Holy Church or Holy
Scripture constitutes the ultimate authority. This is, of course,
one of the fundamental questions posed by the revolt of
Martin Luther and by the Reformation at large.[29]

But how did this fateful dilemma arise? How was this
dichotomy, indeed opposition, of Church and Scripture provoked? To answer this question in adequate fashion is to
examine the whole causal pattern of the Reformation.[30] Within
the scope of this introduction only a brief rejoinder can be
made. The Protestant reformers came to believe that the
existing Church had been utterly corrupted and had de-
parted from the Gospel truth in a most grievous way. Calvin
makes this conviction crystal clear and recounts in detail the
errors and corruptions of which he deems the old Church
guilty. In the second of his speeches before the judgment seat
of God, he describes what may be the process of his own
recognition of error in the old Church and his turning from
it. "My mind being now prepared for serious attention, I at

[28] On Calvin's doctrine of the Church, see Wendel, pp. 291-311. See also
Pontien Polman, *L'Elément historique dans la controverse religieuse du
XVIe siècle* (Gembloux, 1932), pp. 69-94, where the author tends to view
Calvin's appeal to the ancient Church and the Fathers as qualifying his
scriptural principle.

[29] George H. Tavard, *Holy Writ or Holy Church* (London, 1959), ex-
plores this question in terms of the theology and literature of all sides in
the late Middle Ages and the Reformation period. See Ch. VII for Calvin,
pp. 154-56 for reference to Sadoleto's views. See also Robert McAfee Brown,
" 'Tradition' as a Problem for Protestants," *Union Seminary Quarterly Review*, XVI, No. 2 (January 1961), 197-221, for an excellent review article
on Tavard's book.

[30] Tavard does this briefly in so far as the *notion* of 'Scripture alone' and
the relationship of Church and Scripture are concerned. Joseph Lortz,
How the Reformation Came, tr. O. M. Knab (New York, 1964), is a
most suggestive general essay on this causal pattern.

length perceived, as if light had broken in upon me, in what style of error I had wallowed, and how much pollution and impurity I had thereby contracted." One "error" is particularly prominent: the Church's dependence on the "righteousness of works." With this subject broached, we come to the heart of the Reformation controversy, its point of origin as well as the central theological problem it raised. This is the problem of justification, which Calvin in his response to Sadoleto calls "the first and keenest subject of controversy between us."[31]

The experience or "insight" of Luther that man is saved not by his works, but by faith or trust in a merciful God, who, because of Christ's merits, gratuitously imputes justice or righteousness to the sinner, inaugurated his career as reformer and marks the beginning therefore of the Reformation.[32] Formulated as the doctrine of justification by faith alone, it became the basic tenet of Reformation theology. Calvin's conversion, like that of other Protestant reformers and adherents, was essentially the recognition and acceptance of this doctrine and its implications.[33] In view of this, Sadoleto's rather cursory rejection of the Protestant concept of *sola fide* was bound to evoke a fairly extended affirmation of this fundamental belief by Calvin. For Sadoleto the process of justifica-

[31] More extensive Protestant and Catholic statements on this basic problem than can be found in the Sadoleto-Calvin exchange are appended to this volume. This appendix contains (I) Calvin's exposition of the doctrine of justification by faith in the final edition (1559) of his *Institutes of the Christian Religion,* and (II) the decree and the canons concerning justification promulgated at the sixth session of the Council of Trent in January 1547.

[32] Heinrich Boehmer, *Martin Luther: Road to Reformation,* tr. J. W. Doberstein and T. G. Tappert (New York, 1957), Ch. X; Gerhard Ritter, *Luther,* tr. John Riches (New York, 1963), Ch. I. See also Luther's account of this experience in the preface to the edition of his Latin Writing (1545), in *Martin Luther: Selections from His Writings,* ed. John Dillenberger (New York, 1961), pp. 3-12. This account offers an interesting comparison with Calvin's second speech before the judgment seat of God in his reply to Sadoleto.

[33] On Calvin and justification, see Wendel, pp. 255-63; and Wilhelm Niesel, *The Theology of Calvin,* tr. Harold Knight (Philadelphia, 1956), pp. 130-39. The key chapter in the final edition (1559) of the *Institutes* on justification by faith alone is Book III, Ch. XI, wherein Calvin refers to the doctrine as "the main hinge on which religion turns." See Appendix.

tion must encompass good works, and faith, used in the justification formula, must be understood as more than a "mere credulity and confidence in God." It includes "the hope and desire of obeying God, together with love, the head and mistress of all the virtues." Calvin denied that faith here had this broader connotation, and, invoking St. Paul, he restricted it to "a gratuitous promise of divine favor . . . far removed from all works." It is Calvin's conviction that works have no merit or value in justifying a man, although he rejects emphatically Sadoleto's implication that "we leave no room for works." The man who is justified is regenerated and transformed, he says, and will be zealous of doing good.

The exchange does not probe very deeply into this knotty theological problem, although it does present the issue clearly and forcefully. Calvin's reply especially gives a competent statement of the Protestant view, whereas Sadoleto's discussion is very brief and calls for further elucidation. In fact, Sadoleto's explanation of faith and works was questioned at the time by his friend and colleague, Cardinal Contarini, who himself laid greater emphasis on the imputed justice which the Protestants stressed to the exclusion of works.[34] For Catholic theologians and apologists, confronted by the issue as it was raised by Luther and the Protestants, the problem was particularly awkward, and, as Hubert Jedin points out, "there were no ready-made answers at their command."[35] They sought indeed to safeguard man's freedom and cooperation in the process of justification, but the reconciliation of divine grace and human action was not easily made. It was

[34] Douglas, pp. 145-62. Contarini's most important intervention in the justification controversy was in connection with his participation in the Ratisbon Colloquy in 1541. He upheld a doctrine of "double justification" which he erroneously thought would reconcile Rome and Wittenberg, and he elaborated this doctrine in a short treatise, De Justificatione. It received a mixed response from his fellow Catholic theologians. Sadoleto rejected it. On the Ratisbon Colloquy and Contarini, see Pastor, XI, Chs. X and XI, and Heinz Mackensen, "Contarini's Theological Role at Ratisbon in 1541," Archiv für Reformationsgeschichte, LI (1960), No. 1, 36-57.

[35] Hubert Jedin, A History of the Council of Trent, tr. Dom Ernest Graf (2 vols. St. Louis, 1957-61), II, 167. See Pastor, XI, 483.

not until the promulgation of the decree on justification at the Council of Trent in January, 1547, that the Catholic position was authoritatively set forth.[36] Sadoleto was not present at Trent, but we may assume that the doctrine there pronounced won the sincere acceptance of the old Cardinal, "because the Church errs not, and even cannot err, since the Holy Spirit constantly guides her public and universal decrees and Councils."

IV

What result did the correspondence have? Sadoleto's letter led to Calvin's reply, to be sure, but it failed in its main objective to win the Genevans back to the Catholic Church. Written in Latin, it was not widely circulated or popularly available, and its argument apparently had no effect on the city fathers. As a "challenge of the Counter-Reformation," it remained an academic and ineffectual exercise. The magistrates, even though they had ousted Calvin and Farel, continued to uphold the Protestant reforms. The serious division within the Genevan Church and community over the expulsion of the reformers continued until 1540 when the pro-Calvin faction, or *Guillermins*, gained control and sought to induce Calvin to return. In this episode Calvin's reply to Sadoleto, it appears, played a part. His eloquent defense of Protestantism and of his own labors for its establishment in Geneva undoubtedly won him new respect and support in the city.[37] In January, 1540, the Little Council in Geneva authorized Michel du Bois, a local printer, to publish Calvin's reply, a step that has been viewed as marking the decline of

[36] See Appendix. Jedin, II, Chs. V, VII, and VIII, gives an extended account of the prolonged debate that preceded approval of the final decree.

[37] Abroad as well. Luther wrote Bucer in October, 1539, that he read Calvin's reply "with unusual pleasure." It is his only reference in a letter to Calvin by name. Doumergue, II, 571-72.

the anti-Calvin party and leading to the eventual reconciliation of Calvin and Geneva.[38]

This is not to say, however, that Calvin's tract answering Sadoleto was the decisive event in the victory of the *Guillermins* and Calvin's return. The real key to the situation was the opposition that developed in 1539 and 1540 against the anti-Calvin party then in power because of its unsuccessful conduct of negotiations with Bern.[39] In these negotiations over certain jurisdictional rights, arising out of the treaty of August, 1536, between Geneva and Bern, the Genevan representatives abandoned many of the city's claims. Their agreement with Bern was not approved by the Genevan councils, but the scandal of their concessions aroused the city and gave the *Guillermins* broader support as well as new cause for their attack on the government. Tension between the government party, now dubbed the *Articulants* (after the articles of the controversial agreement with Bern), and the *Guillermins* reached fever pitch in the spring of 1540. The arrest and execution of Jean Philippe, leader of the *Articulants,* following a riot in June, signalized the fall of the anti-Calvin party. Soon after, the *Guillermins,* now at the helm, invited Calvin to resume his ministry in their city.[40]

Calvin was not anxious to do so. After his banishment from Geneva, he had taken up residence in Strasbourg at the invitation of Martin Bucer, and his life there was happy, active, and fruitful. He hesitated long before deciding to leave, but at last, yielding to Farel, Viret, and other friends, he agreed to go back. He left Strasbourg for Geneva in September, 1541, and his return to the turbulent city that had once cast him forth begins the great period of Calvin's predominance. Under his leadership Geneva was to become an austere stronghold of Protestant orthodoxy and discipline and the center of the most dynamic movement of the Reformation era. That city

[38] Doumergue, II, 680; Kidd, p. 580.
[39] Walker, pp. 253-58.
[40] Kidd, pp. 586-87.

which Sadoleto sought to restore to the communion of Rome was itself to arise as a second Rome, the saintly city of a vibrant Protestant faith, whose principles of universality and authority were the unique endowment of the exile now returned.[41]

Sadoleto at Carpentras, meanwhile, did not reply to Calvin's public letter. One need not subscribe to Beza's judgment that Calvin wrote "with so much truth and eloquence that Saloleto immediately gave up the whole affair as desperate," but one can speculate that the force and pungency of Calvin's tract dampened his spirits and further depressed his hope for eventual reconciliation and reunion.[42] The appeal he addressed to the Genevans was his last attempt to engage in dialogue with the Protestants. Ironically, it would seem, this attempt contributed to a widening of the breach in Christian Europe. For one thing, it afforded Calvin an opportunity to emerge more distinctly than ever as a forceful defender and champion of Protestant reform.

During 1539 Sadoleto continued work on a treatise on the Church, De christiana ecclesia, in which he emphasized the role of the priesthood and the great need for a faithful and educated clergy.[43] In 1541 he composed a short treatise on justification, taking issue with Contarini's concept of "double justification."[44] Both tracts recall the themes he had advanced in his letter to the Genevans, but he now spoke in the name of reform and doctrinal clarification to his own colleagues within the Church. He remained in his see until early 1542 when the summons of Paul III once more brought him back to Rome. His attention now turned to the preparations for the General Council scheduled to convene soon at Trent.

J. C. O.

---

[41] P. Imbart de la Tour, Calvin et l'Institution chrétienne (Vol. IV of Les Origines de la Réforme. Paris, 1935), pp. 52-53.

[42] Beza's Life of Calvin, loc. cit.

[43] Douglas, pp. 150-52. The text can be found in Angelo Mai, ed., Spicilegium Romanum, II (1839), 101-78.

[44] Douglas, p. 159.

The English translation of both letters presented in this volume is that of Henry Beveridge, published in John Calvin, *Tracts and Treatises on the Reformation of the Church*, Vol. I, by the Calvin Translation Society, Edinburgh, 1844, and reprinted by Wm. B. Eerdmans Publishing Company, Grand Rapids, Mich., 1958. Some slight alteration in spelling, punctuation, and the translation of a few words has been made.

The Latin text of both letters may be found in *Ioannis Calvini opera quae supersunt omnia* (*Corpus Reformatorum*. 59 vols. Brunswick, 1863-1900), V, 369-416.

Both letters were originally published by Wendelin Rihel in Strasbourg in September, 1539. Calvin's translation of both letters into French was published by Michel du Bois in Geneva in 1540. Sadoleto revised his letter for publication by Sebastian Gryphius at Lyons in 1539.

Sadoleto's Letter
to the Genevans

JACOPO SADOLETO, BISHOP OF CARPENTRAS,
CARDINAL PRIEST OF THE CHURCH
OF ST. CALIXTUS,
TO HIS DEARLY BELOVED BRETHREN,
THE MAGISTRATES, COUNCIL, AND CITIZENS OF GENEVA

Very dear brethren in Christ, peace to you and with us, that is, with the Catholic Church, the mother of all, both us and you, love and concord from God, the Father Almighty, and from His only Son Jesus Christ, our Lord, together with the Holy Spirit, perfect Unity in Trinity; to whom be praise and dominion forever and ever. Amen.

I presume, very dear brethren, it is known to some of you that I am now residing at Carpentras, having come from Nice, to which I had attended the Supreme Pontiff on his journey from Rome to mediate between the Kings. For I love this Church and city, which it has pleased God to make my spiritual spouse and country; this my people here I embrace with truly parental affection, and am most reluctant to be separated from them. But should the honor of the Cardinal-ship, which was bestowed upon me unexpectedly, and without my knowledge, oblige me to return to Rome (as it certainly will), that I may there serve in the vocation with which God has called me, it will not withdraw my thoughts and my love from a people who will always remain seated in my inmost heart. Being then at Carpentras, and daily hearing many things of you which excited partly my grief, and partly, too, some hope, leading me not to despond, that you and I, who were formerly in true religion of one mind toward God, might, by the same God looking more benignly upon us, return to the same cordial agreement, it seemed good to the Holy Spirit and to me (for so Scripture speaketh, and assuredly whatsoever things are done with an upright and pious mind toward God are all of the Holy Spirit), it seemed good to me, I say, to write somewhat to you, and declare to you by letter the care and solicitude of mind which I feel for you. For, dearest brethren, this my affection and goodwill toward you is not new, but ever since the time when by the will of God I became Bishop of Carpentras, almost twenty-three years ago, and in consequence of the frequent intercourse between you and my people, had, though absent, learned much of you and your manners, even then began I to love your noble city, the order and form of your republic, the worth of its citizens, and, in particular, that quality lauded and experienced by all, your hospitality to strangers and foreigners; and since vicinity often tends in no small degree to beget love, so in a city contiguous houses, as well as in the world adjacent provinces, lead to regard among neighbors. Before this time, indeed, you happen not to have derived any benefit from this my affection for you, or to have had any sign and indication of it. You never needed my aid, which assuredly would have been most readily given, but hitherto no occasion presented itself to us.

Now, however, of a truth, not only has an opportunity occurred, but necessity is laid upon me to demonstrate in what way I feel affected toward you, if I would maintain my fidelity toward Almighty God, and Christian charity toward my neighbor. For after it was brought to my ears that certain crafty men, enemies of Christian unity and peace, had, in like manner, as they had previously done in some towns and villages of the brave Helvetii, cast among you, and in your city, the wicked seeds of discord, had turned the faithful people of Christ aside from the way of their fathers and ancestors, and from the perpetual sentiments of the Catholic

Church, and filled all places with strife and sedition (such is always the appropriate course of those who seek new power and new honors for themselves, by assailing the authority of the Church), I declare before Almighty God, who is always present beholding my inmost thoughts, that I was exceedingly grieved and affected with a kind of double pity, when, on the one hand, I thought I heard the groans of the Church our mother, weeping and lamenting at being deprived at once of so many and so dear children; and on the other, dearest brethren, I was concerned at your losses and dangers. For well knew I, that such innovators on things ancient and well established, such disturbances, such dissensions, were not only pestiferous to the souls of men (which, however, is the greatest of all evils) but pernicious also to private and public affairs. This you have had the means of learning for yourselves, being instructed by the event. What then? Since my love toward you, and my piety to God, compel me, as a brother to brethren, and friend to friends, freely to lay before you the inmost feelings of my mind, I would earnestly entreat you, that that goodness which you are always wont to evince, you would show to me on the present occasion, by receiving and reading my letter not grudgingly. For I hope that if you will only be pleased to attend impartially to what I write, you will in no small measure approve, if not of my advice, at least of an intention, certainly pure and simple, and above all things desirous of your salvation, and perceive that I am seeking not my own but your good and advantage.

I will not, however, begin with subtle and puzzling disputations, which St. Paul styles philosophy, warning believers in Christ to guard against being deceived by it, and by which those men have misled you, when, among the unwary, they boasted of certain hidden interpretations of Scripture, dignifying their fraud and malice with the noble, indeed, but false and inappropriate, name of learning and wisdom. I will set forth things which are bright and clear, and which have in them no hiding-place of error, no winding of fraud and fallacy; such, indeed, truth always is. For it both shines in darkness, and is perspicuous to every man, and is most easily perceived alike by learned and unlearned, and especially in matters of Christian doctrines, rests not on syllogisms, or quibbles on words, but on humility, reverence, and obedience toward God. For the word of God is quick and powerful, and sharper than any two-edged sword, piercing even to the joinings of soul and spirit, to the inmost parts of the joints and marrow, not ensnaring souls by perplexing argument, but by the inter-position of a certain heavenly affection of the heart, making itself plain and patent to our minds, so that to understand it, it is not so much human reason as God, who calls us to Him-self, and worketh in us. To Him, the Father of all true intel-ligence, I humbly pray that He would, of His goodness, give such assistance to me in speaking, and to you in perceiving, as may again unite us to Himself in one heart and one mind.

And that we may begin with what we deem most season-able, I presume, dearest brethren, that both you and I, and all else besides who have put their faith and hope in Christ, do, and have done so, for this one reason, viz., that they may ob-tain salvation for themselves and their souls—not a salvation which is mortal, and will quickly perish, but one which is ever-during and immortal, which is truly attainable only in heaven, and by no means on earth. Our task, accordingly, is thus divided—having first laid the foundation of faith, we must thereafter labor here in order that we may rest yonder; we must cast seed into the earth, that we may afterward be able to reap in heaven; and in whatever works, or whatever studies we have exercised ourselves here, may ultimately ob-tain similar and fit fruits of our works and labors in another life. And since the way of Christ is arduous, and the method of leading a life conformable to His laws and precepts very difficult (because we are enjoined to withdraw our minds from the contamination of earthly pleasures, and fix them on this one object—to despise the present good which we have in our hands, and aspire to the future, which we see not), still of such value to each one of us is the salvation of himself and of his soul, that we must bring our minds to decline nothing, however harsh, and endure everything, however laborious, that, setting before ourselves the one hope of our salvation, we may at length, through many toils and anxieties (the clemency and mercy of God always taking precedence of our doings), attain to that stable and ever-during salvation.

For this hope, Christ, the herald of the true God, was once received by the world with such universal consent and eagerness; for this reason He is adored and worshipped by us, and truly acknowledged to be God, and the Son of the true God; because, when the minds of men were dead to Almighty God, in whom alone is life, and after living for a little time to the deceitful and fading pleasures of the world, were forthwith doomed utterly and in every part of their nature to destruction, He alone, ever since the world began, awoke them from the dead, that is, from this most fatal kind of death, and first Himself, choosing to be Himself our salvation and deliverance and truth, by submitting to death in the flesh, and shortly after resuming a life no longer mortal, taught and instructed us, by His own example, how, by a way very different from that to which we had been previously accustomed, we should die to this world and the flesh, and live thereafter to God, placing in Him our hopes of living well and happily forever. This is our proper resurrection from the dead—a resurrection truly worthy of the glory and majesty of God Almighty, and by which not one man or two, but the whole human race, are brought back from a dismal and fatal death of the soul to the same soul's true and heavenly life. Paul, setting this kind of resurrection before himself, and beholding in it the greatest sign and proof of the divinity of Christ, says, "I was separated unto the gospel of God, which He had promised by the Prophets in the Holy Scriptures concerning His Son, begotten,

33

indeed, of the seed of David according to the flesh, but determined and declared to be the Son of God in power by the Spirit of holiness"; that is, by spiritual power, which is the proper power of God, because God does His miracles not by body, but by spirit. For His commanding the winds, and by a word restoring sight to the blind, and raising the dead, were done by a power not corporeal but spiritual, which is also divine. Therefore, Christ was declared the Son of God by this spiritual power, which alone is divine, and also, as Paul subjoins, by the resurrection from the dead—not so much that resurrection by which He raised Lazarus, or the widow's son, or the ruler of the synagogue's daughter (although these, too, were works of God), as that by which He delivered Mary Magdalene from seven devils, called Matthew from the receipt of custom, and raised many from an earthly and perishing life; in short, raised the whole human race from sin, and the death of sin, and the power of the darkness of this world, to aspire to, and hope for, light and a celestial relationship— raised up the minds of men when immersed in the mire of earth, and elevated them to heaven. And this greatest benefit of Jesus Christ toward us, and principal proof therein of His divinity, was both instituted by God in the mission of the Son, and undertaken by the Son Himself, and by Him given in its own time, and bestowed upon us, that we, being aided in Christ alone, with all divine and human counsels, helps, and virtues, might present our souls to God in safety. So high is the excellence, so remarkable the price, so great the worth of this thing, viz., the soul of man, that, in order to its not being lost, but gained both to God Himself and to us, the laws of universal nature having been utterly disturbed, and the order of things changed, God descended to the earth, that He might become man, and man was raised to heaven, that he might be a God.

We all, therefore, (as I said) believe in Christ in order that we may find salvation for our souls, i.e., life for ourselves:

than this there can be nothing more earnestly to be desired, no blessing more internal, more close and familiar to us. For in proportion to the love which each man bears to himself is his salvation dear to him; if it be neglected and cast away, what prize, pray, of equal value can possibly be acquired? What will a man give in exchange for his soul? saith the Lord; or what will it profit a man should he gain the whole world, and lose his own soul? This possession, therefore, so large, so dear, so precious to every man as is his soul, we must use every effort to retain; since all the other blessings which we desire are external, and alien to us, this one good of a preserved soul is not only ours, but truly we ourselves are that very good. He who has neglected and lost it will not be able to have any other good which he can enjoy, the very being who ought to enjoy it having already lost himself.

Moreover, we obtain this blessing of complete and perpetual salvation by faith alone in God and in Jesus Christ. When I say by faith alone, I do not mean, as those inventors of novelties do, a mere credulity and confidence in God, by which, to the seclusion of charity and the other duties of a Christian mind, I am persuaded that in the cross and blood of Christ all my faults are unknown; this indeed is necessary, and forms the first access which we have to God, but it is not enough. For we must also bring a mind full of piety toward Almighty God, and desirous of performing whatever is agreeable to Him; in this, especially, the power of the Holy Spirit resides. This mind, though sometimes it proceeds not to external acts, is, however, inwardly prepared of itself for well-doing and shows a prompt desire to obey God in all things, and this in us is the true habit of divine justice. For what else does this name of justice signify, or what other meaning and idea does it present to us, if regard is not had in it to good works? For Scripture says, that "God sent his Son to prepare a people acceptable to Himself, zealous of good works"; and in another place it says, that we may be built up in Christ unto good works. If, then, Christ was sent that we, by well-doing, may, through Him, be accepted of God, and that we may be built up in Him unto good works; surely the faith which we have in God through Jesus Christ not only enjoins and commands us to confide in Christ but to confide, working or resolved to work well in Him. For faith is a term of full and ample signification, and not only includes in it credulity and confidence, but also the hope and desire of obeying God, together with love, the head and mistress of all the virtues, as has been most clearly manifested to us in Christ, in which love the Holy Spirit properly and peculiarly resides, or rather Himself is love, since God is love. Wherefore, as without the Holy Spirit, so also without love, nought of ours is pleasing and acceptable to God. When we say, then, that we can be saved by faith alone in God and Jesus Christ, we hold that in this very faith love is essentially comprehended as the chief and primary cause of our salvation.

But to leave off disputation, and return to where we left; we have shown you, dearest brethren, or, rather, attempted to show (for our discourse is not equal to the magnitude of the subject), how important it is, how deeply it concerns us to secure our soul and its salvation, because our soul is our whole selves, is properly our good and only good, while all other goods are foreign to us, and disjoined from us, and cannot in any degree be enjoyed, if we fail of obtaining this, which is first and truly ours. In order to defend and preserve the interest of their souls, so many most glorious martyrs of Christ in former times have cheerfully laid down this mortal life; so many most holy doctors have made it their business to toil and watch, day and night, that they might lead us into the right way, and establish us in it; the whole Church once endured so many and so grievous injuries and calamities from impious tyrants and governors. All these things, accordingly, were permitted by Almighty God, and were undertaken, endured, and warred by those brave men, true worshippers of

Christ, that the Church being, by means of every kind of experiment and trial, beaten, as it were, with numbers of hammers, purified with much fire, heated, melted, consolidated, and worked into shape by so many toils and labors of saints, might for her fidelity obtain the highest favor with God, and the greatest authority among men. This Church hath regenerated us to God in Christ, hath nourished and confirmed us, instructed us what to think, what to believe, wherein to place our hope, and also taught us by what way we must tend toward heaven. We walk in this common faith of the Church, we retain her laws and precepts. And if, at any time, overcome by frailty and inconstancy, we lapse into sin (would that this happened to us rarely at least, and not too often), we, however, rise again in the same faith of the Church; and by whatever expiations, penances, and satisfactions, she tells us that our sin is washed away, and we (always by the grace and mercy of God) restored to our former integrity, these methods of expiation and satisfaction we have recourse to and employ —trusting, when we do so, to find a place of mercy and pardon with God. For we do not arrogate to ourselves anything beyond the opinion and authority of the Church; we do not persuade ourselves that we are wise above what we ought to be; we do not show our pride in contemning the decrees of the Church; we do not make a display among the people of towering intellect or ingenuity, or some new wisdom; but (I speak of true and honest Christians) we proceed in humility and in obedience, and the things delivered to us, and fixed by the authority of our ancestors (men of the greatest wisdom and holiness), we receive with all faith, as truly dictated and enjoined by the Holy Spirit.

For we know and are assured how great power, how great importance, how great weight, humility has with God—humility, a virtue peculiarly Christian, which Christ our Lord always brought particularly forward in his admonitions and precepts, and acts and miracles, declaring that for little ones only, that is, the humble, the kingdom of heaven is prepared. For it makes no difference whether we be small or great in stature, but it makes the greatest difference whether we be of a humble or of a haughty mind. The same pride which cast down the angels from heaven impedes men in their journey toward heaven. To that place whence the angel, a heavenly creature, was expelled because of pride, man, a creature of the earth, is exalted because of humility, making it plainly appear that humility constitutes both the chief help to our eternal salvation, and the chief support of that sweet and blessed hope with which we tend heavenward.

Since these things are so, dearest brethren, since our salvation, since true life, since eternal felicity, since ourselves, in short, ought to be, in the first place, and above all things, dear to us, since if we lose ourselves we shall nevermore find anything that is truly ours, that is, to delight or belong to us, since no heavier loss, no more fatal evil, no more dreadful calamity, can befall us than the loss and perdition of our souls, with how great zeal, I ask, with what care and anxiety of mind, ought we to guard against exposing our life and salvation to this great danger? You will surely grant and concede to me, that nothing more pernicious and fearful can happen to anyone than the loss of his soul. I presume you will therefore grant also that there is no event against the occurrence of which we ought to guard with greater zeal and diligence. For when an evil, if it befalls us, is the worst of all evils, the danger of that evil ought to be dreaded by us as the most fearful of all dangers. The greater the extent of the evil, the greater must be our fear when exposed to it. And as those who fear and shudder at being precipitated into the sea do not even venture to approach any steep rock hanging over the sea, so those who tremble at the dreadful condemnatory sentence of God flee above all things from the danger which comes nearest and closest to that eternal misery. Nor do I here at this time maintain that all do not sin, and that as long as we are in this life we are not all of us in danger (plainly we are so; we all go astray, and stumble, and fall, sometime oftener, sometime more seldom, as each possesses in himself, and from God, the virtue of self-restraint); nevertheless, other sins, those especially which are done and committed not of fixed purpose, but through frailty, have an easy return to the mercy of Almighty God; but that horrid and dreadful sin, by which depraved worship is offered to God, who ought to be most purely worshipped, and by which false things are thought of Him, the Supreme and only Truth, this, this, I say, is a sin which not only places us in the most immediate peril of eternal death, but also leaves us almost without hope and endeavor to turn aside and shun the peril. For, in our other sins, which are like the billows of life, the anchor of our ship is still safe to keep us from rocks and shipwreck, because we turn our thoughts from time to time toward God, and, stung with compunction for sin, we, with silent groans, and with confession of our iniquity, implore His mercy. And He, as He is full of goodness and clemency, is instantly inclined to pardon, and, after the manner of an affectionate parent, listens appeased to the prayer of His children. But in this deep and dreadful sin of preposterous and false religion, we no longer leave to ourselves either God or anchor. Wherefore, dearest brethren, if we would be safe, this danger, in particular, we must most carefully and studiously shun.

It may here be said, that since, in regard to what constitutes corrupt or genuine religion, judgments vary; and the opinions of men, especially at this time, are different, one interpreting in this way, and another in that, it would seem to be enough if anyone, with sincere mind, adopts the belief which is first presented to him, and submits his own judgment to the judgment of those better skilled and learned than himself. I admit, dearest brethren, that these are the words of simple men, and of men who are by nature of duller intellect (those who twist and turn them aside from the right path have the greater sin), for this language is not suited to the wise and wary. But let me now, for the time, admit that these things are uncertain to all, both learned and unlearned (though it is far otherwise, for the Catholic Church has a certain rule by which to discriminate between truth and falsehood); however, let us grant that they are doubtful; since the point in question is jeopardy to our salvation; since we set the highest value upon our souls, i.e., ourselves; and since it is not our fortune or our health, or even our body and this mortal life, which are at stake (the loss of all which brave men have often suffered with constancy for Christ and their soul), but the point to be decided is whether we are to live eternally most miserable, or most blessed—it behooves us to look around, consider and diligently weigh how we may establish ourselves (I speak of the thing as doubtful, though, however, it is not); how, I say, we may stand, where the least fear and danger, and the greatest hope and security appear.

No man, I believe, will deny me this much, that in a matter dubious and uncertain (one, especially, where the whole of life and salvation is concerned), we ought rather to adopt and follow the counsel which reason gives than that which fortuitous rashness casts in our way. Let us see then in which party, and in which sect, there is the greatest danger of removing farther from God, and moving nearer to endless destruction. This point I will treat and expound, as if I saw you still deliberating and not yet certain whose wishes you ought in preference to follow, or in whose counsels confide.

The point in dispute is whether is it more expedient for your salvation, and whether you think you will do what is more pleasing to God, by believing and following what the Catholic Church throughout the whole world, now for more than fifteen hundred years, or (if we require clear and certain recorded notice of the facts) for more than thirteen hundred years approves with general consent; or innovations introduced within these twenty-five years, by crafty or, as they think themselves, acute men; but men certainly who are not themselves the Catholic Church? For, to define it briefly, the Catholic Church is that which in all parts, as well as at the present time in every region of the world, united and consenting in Christ, has been always and everywhere directed by the one Spirit of Christ; in which Church no dissension can exist; for all its parts are connected with each other, and breathe together. But should any dissension and strife arise, the great body of the Church indeed remains the same, but an abscess is formed by which some corrupted flesh, being torn off, is separated from the spirit which animates the body, and no longer belongs in substance to the body ecclesiastic. I will not here descend to the discussion of single points, or load your ears with a multitude of words and arguments. I will say nothing of the Eucharist, in which we worship the most true body of Christ. Those men, little aware how in each kind of learning it is necessary to employ reasons and arguments, endeavor, by means of reasons which are inapplicable, and drawn from dialectics and vain philosophy, to enclose the very Lord of the universe, and His divine and spiritual power therein (which is altogether free and infinite), within the corners of a corporeal nature, circumscribed by its own boundaries. Nor will I speak of confession of sins to a priest, in which confession that which forms the strongest foundation of our safety, viz., true Christian humility, has both been demonstrated by Scripture, and established and enjoined by the Church; this humility these men have studied calumniously to evade, and presumptuously to cast away. Nor will I say anything either of the prayers of the saints to God for us, or of ours for the dead, though I would fain know what these same men would be at when they despise and deride them. Can they possibly imagine that the soul perishes along with its body? This they certainly seem to insinuate, and they do it still more openly when they strive to procure for themselves a liberty of conduct set loose from all ecclesiastical laws, and a license for their lusts. For if the soul is mortal, let us eat and drink, says the Apostle, for tomorrow we die; but if it is immortal, as it certainly is, how, I ask, has the death of the body made so great and so sudden a disruption that the souls of the dead have no congruity in any respect, no communion with those of the living, and have forgotten all their relationship to us and common human society? and this, especially, while charity, which is the principal gift of the Holy Spirit to a Christian soul, which is ever kind, ever fruitful, and which, in him who has it, never exists to no purpose, must always remain safe and operative in both lives.

But to leave off controversies, and reserve them for their own time, let us discuss what was first proposed—let us inquire and see which of the two is more conducive to our advantage, and which is better in itself, and better fitted to obtain the favor of Almighty God, whether to accord with the whole Church, and faithfully observe her decrees, and laws, and sacraments, or to assent to men seeking dissension and novelty. This is the place, dearest brethren, this the highway where the road breaks off in two directions, the one of which leads us to life, and the other to everlasting death. On this discrimination and choice, the salvation of every man's soul, the pledges of future life, are at stake—whether is our lot to be one of eternal felicity, or of infinite misery? What, then, shall we say? Let us here suppose two persons, one of each class, that is, from each road; let them be placed before the dread tribunal of the sovereign Judge; and there let their case be examined and weighed, in order to ascertain whether a condemnatory or a saving sentence can justly be pronounced. They will be interrogated whether they were Christians. Both will say that they were. Whether they properly believed in Christ? Both will, in like manner, answer yea. But when they will be examined as to what they believed, and how they believed (for this investigation, respecting right faith, precedes that concerning life and character), when a confession of right faith will be exacted of them, he who was educated in the lap and discipline of the Catholic Church will say:

"Having been instructed by my parents, who had learned it from their fathers and forefathers, that I should, in all things, be obedient to the Catholic Church, and revere and observe its laws, admonitions, and decrees, as if Thou, thyself, O Lord, hadst made them, and perceiving that almost all who bore the Christian name and title in our days, and before it, and followed Thy standards far and wide over the world, were and had been of the same opinion, all of them acknowledging and venerating this very Church, as the mother of their faith, and regarding it as a kind of sacrilege to depart from her precepts and constitution, I studied to approve myself to Thee by the same faith which the Catholic Church keeps and inculcates. And though new men had come with the Scripture much in their mouths and hands, who attempted to stir some novelties, to pull down what was ancient, to argue against the Church, to snatch away and wrest from us the obedience which we all yielded to it, I was still desirous to adhere firmly to that which had been delivered to me by my parents, and observed from antiquity, with the consent of most holy and most learned Fathers; and although the actual manners of many prelates and ecclesiastics were such as might move my indignation, I did not, therefore, abandon my sentiments. For I concluded, that it was my duty to obey their precepts, which were certainly holy, as Thou, God, hadst commanded in Thy Gospel, while Thou behoovedst to be the only Judge of their life and actions; and, especially, since I was myself stained by the many sins which were manifest to Thee on my forehead, I could not be a fit judge of others. For these sins, I now stand before Thy tribunal, imploring not strict justice, O Lord, but rather Thy mercy and readiness to forgive."

Thus will this one plead his cause.

The other will be summoned and will appear. He will be commanded to speak. Supposing him to be one of those who are, or have been, the authors of dissension, he will thus begin his oration:

"Almighty God, when I beheld the manners of ecclesiastics almost everywhere corrupt, and saw the priests, nevertheless, from a regard to religion, universally honored, offended at their wealth, a just indignation, as I consider it, inflamed my mind, and made me their opponent; and when I beheld myself, after having devoted so many years to literature and theology, without that place in the Church which my labors had merited, while I saw many unworthy persons exalted to honors and priestly offices, I betook myself to the assailing of those who I thought were by no means pleasing and acceptable to Thee. And because I could not destroy their power without first trampling on the laws enacted by the Church, I induced a great part of the people to contemn those rights of the Church which had long before been ratified and inviolate. If these had been decreed in General Councils, I said we were not to yield to the authority of Councils; if they had been instituted by ancient Fathers and Doctors, I accused the old Fathers as unskillful and devoid of sound understanding; if by Roman Pontiffs, I affirmed that they had raised up a tyranny for themselves, and falsely assumed the name of Viceregents of Christ: by all means, in short, I contended that all of us, Thy worshippers, should shake off the tyrannical yoke of the Church, which sometimes forbids meats, which observes days, which will have us to confess our sins to priests, which orders vows to be performed, and which binds with so many chains of bondage men made free, O Christ, in Thee; and that we should trust to faith alone, and not also to good works (which are particularly extolled and proclaimed in the Church), to procure us righteousness and salvation—seeing, especially, that Thou hadst paid the penalty for us, and by Thy sacred blood wiped away all faults and crimes, in order that we, trusting to this our faith in Thee, might thereafter be able to do, with greater freedom, whatsoever we listed. For I searched the

Scriptures more ingeniously than those ancients did, and that more especially when I sought for something which I might wrest against them. Having thus by repute for learning and genius acquired fame and estimation among the people, though, indeed, I was not able to overturn the whole authority of the Church, I was, however, the author of great seditions and schisms in it."

After he has thus spoken, and spoken truly (for there is no room to lie before that heavenly Judge, though he has kept back much concerning his ambition, avarice, love of popular applause, inward fraud and malice, of which he is perfectly conscious, and which will appear inscribed on his very forehead), I ask you, my Genevese brethren, whom I long to have of one mind with me in Christ, and in the Church of Christ, what judgment, think you, will be passed on these two men and their associates and followers? Is it not certain that he who followed the Catholic Church will not be judged guilty of any error in this respect? First, because the Church errs not, and even cannot err, since the Holy Spirit constantly guides her public and universal decrees and Councils. Secondly, even if she did err, or could have erred (this, however, it is impious to say or believe), no such error would be condemned in him who should, with a mind sincere and humble toward God, have followed the faith and authority of his ancestors. But the other, trusting to his own head, having none among the ancient Fathers, and not even general assemblies of the whole Bishops, whom he deems worthy of honor, and to whom he can bring his mind to yield and submit, arrogating all things to himself, more prepared to slander than to speak or teach, after revolting from the common Church, to what does he look as the haven of his fortunes? in what bulwark does he confide? to whom does he trust as his advocates with God, so as not to have great cause of dread that he will be cast into outer darkness, where there will be weeping and gnashing of teeth, that is, where he will forever lament his miseries, and gnash with his teeth against himself, because when it was in his power, if he had chosen, to avoid that most dreadful calamity, he had neglected to do so? Every person can understand for himself what wretched and dismal companions grief and fury are to pass one's life with, especially when there will never be any end or any limit of the fatal loss—when weeping and wrath shall never cease.

But if all other things might in some way be tolerated and overlooked, how will this be borne (for this, methinks, there cannot be with God any place for mercy and pardon), that they attempted to tear the spouse of Christ in pieces, that that garment of the Lord, which heathen soldiers were unwilling to divide, they attempted not only to divide, but to rend? For already, since these men began, how many sects have torn the Church? sects not agreeing with them, and yet disagreeing with each other—a manifest indication of falsehood, as all doctrine declares. Truth is always one, while falsehood is varied and multiform; that which is straight is simple, that which is crooked has many turns. Can anyone who acknowledges and confesses Christ, and into whose heart and mind the Holy Spirit hath shone, fail to perceive that such rending, such tearing of the holy Church, is the proper work of Satan, and not of God? What does God demand of us? What does Christ enjoin? That we be all one in Him. Why was given us from heaven that singular and pre-eminent gift of love, a gift divinely implanted in the Christian race only, and not in other nations? Was it not that we might all confess the Lord with one heart and mouth? Do those men suppose that the Christian religion is anything at all but peace with God, and concord with our neighbor? Let us see what the Lord Himself says in John, when interceding with His Father for the disciples: "Holy Father, keep in thy name those whom thou hast given me, that they may be one as we are: I ask not for them only, but for those also who are to believe in me through their word; that they all may be one;

as thou, Father, art in me, and I in thee, that they too may be one in us: that the world may believe that thou hast sent me. And the glory which thou gavest me I have given them; that they may be one, as we also are one: I in them, and thou in me, that they may be perfected into one." You see, dearest brethren, and in the clear light of the gospel discern what it really is to be a Christian, since our faith toward God, and all the glory of God, both His with us, and ours with Him, consists solely in this unity; since this is the only thing which Christ requires and asks of the Father concerning us—considering that His labors, His toils, His frail human body assumed for us, His cross and His death will produce fruit, both to the glory of God (His first desire), and to our salvation (for which He was about to die), if we shall be one among ourselves, and one in Him. For this the Catholic Church always labors, for this she strives, viz., our concord and unity in the same Spirit, that all men, however divided by space or time, and so incapable of coming together as one body, may yet be both cherished and ruled by one Spirit, who is always and everywhere the same. To this Catholic Church and Holy Spirit those, on the contrary, are professed adversaries who attempt to break unity, to introduce various spirits, to dissolve consent, and banish concord from the Christian religion, attempting this, with an eagerness and a zeal, by machinations and arts, which no language can sufficiently express. I will not, indeed, pray against them that the Lord would destroy all deceitful lips and high-sounding tongues; nor, likewise, that He would add iniquity to their iniquity, but that He would convert them, and bring them to a right mind, I will earnestly entreat of the Lord, my God, as I now do.

And I beg and exhort you, my Genevese brethren, after the mists of error have at length cleared away from the eyes of your mind, and the light been displayed, that you would raise your eyes to that heaven which God has set before you as your everlasting country, that you would be pleased to return to concord with us, yield faithful homage to the Church, our mother, and worship God with us in one spirit. Nor if our manners perhaps displease you, if by the fault of some that splendor of the Church, which ought to be perpetual and untarnished, is somewhat obscured, let that move your minds, or draw you to a different or opposite party. You may, perhaps, hate our persons (if the gospel allows it), but you certainly ought not to have a hatred for our faith and doctrine; for it is written, "What they say, do." Now, we say nothing more than express our eager desire for your salvation. If this, my dearest Genevese, shall be taken by you in good part, if you will listen favorably to one most desirous of your welfare, assuredly you will not repent of having recovered your former favor with God and praise with men. I, as is my part, and as my goodwill toward you dictates, will be a constant suppliant to God for you—an unworthy one, indeed, through my own defects, but perhaps love will make me worthy. And then, whatever I possibly can do, although it is very small, still if I have in me any talent, skill, authority, industry, I make a tender of all to you and your interests, and will regard it as a great favor to myself, should you be able to reap any fruit and advantage from my labor, and assistance in things human and divine.

It only remains to beg of you to receive the messenger, who bears this letter to you, with the civility and kindness which your own humanity and the law of nations, and, above all, Christian meekness, require and demand. While this will be honorable to you, it will also be extremely agreeable to me. God guide and mercifully defend you, my dearest brethren.

Carpentras, March 18, 1539

Calvin's Reply to Sadoleto

JOHN CALVIN

TO

JACOPO SADOLETO, CARDINAL,

GREETINGS.

In the great abundance of learned men whom our ages has produced, your excellent learning and distinguished eloquence having deservedly procured you a place among the few whom all, who would be thought studious of liberal arts, look up to and revere, it is with great reluctance I bring forward your name before the learned world, and address to you the following expostulation. Nor, indeed, would I have done it if I had not been dragged into this arena by a strong necessity. For I am not unaware how reprehensible it would be to show any eagerness in attacking a man who has deserved so well of literature, nor how odious I should become to all the learned were they to see me stimulated by passion merely, and not impelled by any just cause, turning my pen against one whom, for his admirable endowments, they, not without good reason, deem worthy of love and honor. I trust, however, that after explaining the nature of my undertaking, I shall not only be exempted from all blame, but there will not be an individual who will not admit that the cause which I have undertaken I could not on any account have abandoned without basely deserting my duty.

You lately addressed a letter to the Senate and people of Geneva, in which you sounded their inclination as to whether, after having once shaken off the yoke of the Roman Pontiff, they would submit to have it again imposed upon them. In that letter, as it was not expedient to wound the feelings of those whose favor you required to gain your cause, you acted the part of a good pleader; for you endeavored to soothe them by abundance of flattery, in order that you might gain them over to your views. Any thing of obloquy and bitterness you directed against those whose exertions had produced the revolt from that tyranny. And here (so help you) you bear down full sail upon those who, under pretense of the gospel, have by wicked arts urged on the city to what you deplore as the subversion of religion and of the Church. I, however, Sadoleto, profess to be one of those whom with so much enmity you assail and stigmatise. For though religion was already established, and the form of the Church corrected, before I was invited to Geneva, yet having not only approved by my suffrage, but studied as much as in me lay to preserve and confirm what had been done by Viret and Farel, I cannot separate my case from theirs. Still, if you had attacked me in my private character, I could easily have forgiven the attack in consideration of your learning, and in honor of letters. But when I see that my ministry, which I feel assured is supported and sanctioned by a call from God, is wounded through my side, it would be perfidy, not patience, were I here to be silent and connive.

In that Church I have held the office first of Doctor, and then of Pastor. In my own right, I maintain that in undertaking these offices I had a legitimate vocation. How faithfully and religiously I have performed them, there is no occasion for now showing at length. Perspicuity, erudition, prudence, ability, not even industry, will I now claim for myself, but that I certainly labored with the sincerity which became me in the work of the Lord, I can in conscience appeal to Christ, my Judge, and all His angels, while all good men bear clear testimony in my favor. This ministery, therefore, when it shall appear to have been of God (as it certainly shall appear, after the cause has been heard), were I in silence to allow you to tear and defame, who would not condemn such silence as treachery? Every person, therefore, now sees that the strongest obligations of duty—obligations which I cannot evade—constrain me to meet your accusations, if I would not with manifest perfidy desert and betray a cause with which the Lord has entrusted me.

For though I am for the present relieved of the charge of the Church of Geneva, that circumstance ought not to prevent me from embracing it with paternal affection—God, when He gave it to me in charge, having bound me to be faithful to it for ever. Now, then, when I see the worst snares laid for that Church whose safety it has pleased the Lord to make my highest care, and grievous peril impending if not obviated, who will advise me to await the issue silent and unconcerned? How heartless, I ask, would it be to wink in idleness, and, as it were, vacillating at the destruction of one whose life you are bound vigilantly to guard and preserve? But more on this point were superfluous, since you yourself relieve me of all difficulty. For if neighborhood, and that not very near, has weighed so much with you, that while wishing to profess your love towards the Genevese, you hesitate not so bitterly to assail me and my fame, it will undoubtedly, by the law of humanity, be conceded to me, while desiring to consult for the public good of a city entrusted to me by a far stronger obligation than that of neighborhood, to oppose your counsels and endeavors which I cannot doubt tend to its destruction. Besides, without paying the least regard to the Genevan Church (though assuredly I cannot cast off that charge anymore than that of my own soul), supposing I were not actuated by any zeal for it, still, when my ministry (which, knowing it to be from Christ, I am bound, if need be, to maintain with my blood) is assailed and falsely traduced, how can it be lawful for me to bear it as if I saw it not?

Wherefore, it is easy not only for impartial readers to judge, but for yourself, also, Sadoleto, to consider how numerous and valid the reasons are which have compelled me to engage in this contest, if the name of contest should be given to a simple and dispassionate defense of my innocence against your calumnious accusations. I say *my* innocence, although I cannot plead for myself without, at the same time, including my colleagues, with whom all my measures in that administration were so conjoined, that whatever has been said against them I willingly take to myself. What the feelings are which I have had toward yourself in undertaking this cause, I will study to testify and prove by my mode of conducting it. For I will act so that all may perceive that I have not only greatly the advantage of you in the goodness and justice of the cause, in conscientious rectitude, heartfelt sincerity, and candor of speech, but have also been considerably more successful in maintaining gentleness and moderation. There will doubtless be some things which will sting, or, it may be, speak daggers to your mind, but it will be my endeavor, first, not to allow any harsher expression to escape me than either the injustice of the accusations with which you have previously assailed me, or the necessity of the case may extort; and, secondly, not to allow any degree of harshness which may amount to intemperance or passion, or which may, by its appearance of petulance, give offense to ingenuous minds.

And, first, if you had to do with any other person, he would, undoubtedly, begin with the very argument which I have determined altogether to omit. For, without much ado, he would discuss your design in writing, until he should make it plain that your object was anything but what you profess it to be. For were it not for the great credit you formerly acquired for candor, it is somewhat suspicious that a stranger, who never before had any intercourse with the Genevese, should now suddenly profess for them so great an affection, though no previous sign of it existed, while as one imbued, almost from a boy, with Romish arts (such arts as are now learned in the Court of Rome, that forge of all craft and trickery), educated, too, in the very bosom of Clement, and now, moreover, elected a cardinal, you have many things about you which, with most men, would in this matter subject you to suspicion. Then as to those insinuations by which you have supposed you might win your way into the minds of simple men, anyone, not utterly stupid, might easily refute them. But things of this nature, though many will, perhaps, be disposed to believe them, I am unwilling to ascribe to you, because they seem to me unsuitable to the character of one who has been polished by all kinds of liberal learning. I will, therefore, in entering into discussion with you, give you credit for having written to the Genevese with the purest intention as becomes one of your learning, prudence, and gravity, and for having, in good faith, advised them to the course which you believed conducive to their interest and safety. But whatever may have been your intention (I am unwilling, in this matter, to charge you with anything invidious), when, with the bitterest and most contumelious expressions which you can employ, you distort, and endeavor utterly to destroy what the Lord delivered by our hands, I am compelled, whether I will or not, to withstand you openly. For then only do pastors edify the Church, when, besides leading docile souls to Christ placidly, as with the hand, they are also armed to repel the machinations of those who strive to impede the work of God.

Although your letter has many windings, its whole purport substantially is to recover the Genevese to the power of the Roman Pontiff, or to what you call the faith and obedience of the Church. But as, from the nature of the case, their feelings required to be softened, you preface with a long oration concerning the incomparable value of eternal life. You afterward come nearer to the point, when you show that there is nothing more pestiferous to souls than a perverse worship of God; and again, that the best rule for the due worship of God is that which is prescribed by the Church, and that, therefore, there is no salvation for those who have violated the unity of the Church unless they repent. But you next contend that separation from your fellowship is manifest revolt from the Church, and then that the gospel which the Genevese received from us is nothing but a large farrago of impious dogmas. From this you infer what kind of divine judgment awaits them if they attend not to your admonitions. But as it was of the greatest importance to your cause to throw complete discredit on our words, you labor to the utmost to fill them with sinister suspicions of the zeal which they saw us manifest for their salvation. Accordingly, you captiously allege that we had no other end in view than to gratify our avarice and ambition. Since, then, your device has been to cast some stain upon us, in order that the minds of your readers, being preoccupied with hatred might give us no credit, I will, before proceeding to other matters, briefly reply to that objection.

I am unwilling to speak of myself, but since you do not permit me to be altogether silent, I will say what I can consistent with modesty. Had I wished to consult my own interest, I would never have left your party. I will not, indeed, boast that there the road to preferment had been easy to me. I never desired it, and I could never bring my mind to catch at it; although I certainly know not a few of my own age who have crept up to some eminence—among them some whom I might have equalled, and others outstripped. This only I will be contented to say, it would not have been difficult for me to reach the summit of my wishes, viz., the enjoyment of literary ease with something of a free and honorable station. Therefore, I have no fear that anyone not possessed of shameless effrontery will object to me that out of the kingdom of the Pope I sought for any personal advantage which was not there ready to my hand.

And who dare object this to Farel? Had it been necessary for him to live by his own industry, he had already made attainments in literature, which would not have allowed him to suffer want, and he was of a more distinguished family than to require external aid. As to those of us to whom you pointed as with the finger, it seemed proper for us to reply in our own name. But since you seem to throw out indirect insinuations against all who in the present day are united with us in sustaining the same cause, I would have you understand that not one can be mentioned for whom I cannot give you a better answer than for Farel and myself. Some of our [reformers] are known to you by fame. As to them, I appeal to your own conscience. Think you it was hunger which drove them away from you, and made them in despair flee to that change as a means of bettering their fortunes? But not to go over a long catalogue, this I say, that of those who first engaged in this cause, there was none who with you might not have been in better place and fortune than require on such grounds to look out for some new plan of life.

But come and consider with me for a little what the honors and powers are which we have gained. All our hearers will bear us witness that we did not covet or aspire to any other riches or dignities than those which fell to our lot. Since in all our words and deeds they not only perceived no trace of the ambition with which you charge us, but, on the contrary, saw clear evidence of our abhorring it with our whole heart, you cannot hope that by one little word their minds are to be so fascinated as to credit a futile slander in opposition to the many certain proofs with which we furnished them. And to appeal to facts rather than words, the power of the sword, and other parts of civil jurisdiction, which bishops and priests under the semblance of immunity had wrested from the magistrate and claimed for themselves, have not we restored to the magistrate? All their usurped instruments of tyranny and ambition have not we detested and struggled to abolish?

If there was any hope of rising, why did we not craftily dissemble, so that those powers might have passed to us along with the office of governing the Church? And why did we make such exertion to overturn the whole of that dominion, or rather butchery, which they exercised upon souls, without any sanction from the Word of God? How did we not consider that it was just so much lost to ourselves? In regard to ecclesiastical revenues, they are still in a great measure swallowed up by these whirlpools. But if there was a hope that they will one day be deprived of them (as at length they certainly must), why did we not devise a way by which they might come to us? But when with clear voice we denounced as a thief any bishop who, out of ecclesiastical revenues, appropriated more to his own use than was necessary for a frugal and sober subsistence; when we protested that the Church was exposed to a deadly poison, so long as pastors were loaded with an affluence under which they themselves might ultimately sink; when we declared it inexpedient that these revenues should fall into their possession; finally, when we counselled that as much should be distributed to ministers as might suffice for a frugality befitting their order, not superabound for luxury, and that the rest should be dispensed according to the practice of the ancient Church; when we showed that men of weight ought to be elected to manage these revenues, under an obligation to account annually to the Church and the magistracy, was this to entrap any of these for ourselves, or was it not rather voluntarily to shake ourselves free of them? All these things, indeed, demonstrate not what we are, but what we wished to be. But if these things are so plainly and generally known that not one iota can be denied, with what face can you proceed to upbraid us with aspiring to extraordinary wealth and power, and this especially in the presence of men to whom none of those things are unknown? The monstrous lies which persons of your order spread against us among their own followers we are not surprised at (for no man is present who can either reprimand or venture to refute them), but where men have been eyewitnesses of all the things which we have above mentioned, to try to persuade them of the contrary is the part of a man of little discretion, and strongly derogates from Sadoleto's reputation for learning, prudence, and gravity. But if you think that our intention must be judged by the result, it will be found that the only thing we aimed at was that the kingdom of Christ might be promoted by our poverty and insignificance. So far are we from having abused His sacred name to purposes of ambition.

I pass in silence many other invectives which you thunder out against us (open-mouthed, as it is said). You call us crafty men, enemies of Christian unity and peace, innovators on things ancient and well-established, seditious, alike pestiferous to souls, and destructive both publicly and privately to society at large. Had you wished to escape rebuke, you either ought not, for the purpose of exciting prejudice, to have attributed to us a magniloquent tongue, or you ought to have kept your own magniloquence considerably more under check. I am unwilling, however, to dwell on each of these points; only I would have you to consider how unbecoming, not to say illiberal, it is thus in many words to accuse the innocent of things which by one word can be instantly refuted; although to inflict injury on man is a small matter when compared with the indignity of that contumely, which, when you come to the question, you offer to Christ and His Word. When the Genevese, instructed by our preaching, escaped from the gulf of error in which they were immersed, and betook themselves to a purer teaching of the gospel, you call it defection from the truth of God; when they threw off the tyranny of the Roman Pontiff, in order that they might establish among themselves a better form of Church, you call it a desertion from the Church. Come, then, and let us discuss both points in their order.

As to your preface, which, in proclaiming the excellence of eternal blessedness, occupies about a third part of your letter, it cannot be necessary for me to dwell long in reply. For although commendation of the future and eternal life is a theme which deserves to be sounded in our ears by day and by night, to be constantly kept in remembrance, and made the subject of ceaseless meditation, yet I know not for what reason you have so spun out your discourse upon it here, unless it were to recommend yourself by giving some indication of religious feeling. But whether, in order to remove all doubt concerning yourself, you wished to testify that a life of glory seriously occupies your thoughts, or whether you supposed that those to whom you wrote required to be excited and spurred on by a long commendation of it (for I am unwilling to divine what your intention may have been), it is not very sound theology to confine a man's thoughts so much to himself, and not to set before him, as the prime motive of his existence, zeal to illustrate the glory of God. For we are born first of all for God, and not for ourselves. As all things flowed from Him, and subsist in Him, so, says Paul, (Rom. xi. 36) they ought to be referred to Him. I acknowledge, indeed, that the Lord, the better to recommend the glory of His name to men, has tempered zeal for the promotion and extension of it, by uniting it indissolubly with our salvation. But since He has taught that this zeal ought to exceed all thought and care for our own good and advantage, and since natural equity also teaches that God does not receive what is His own, unless He is preferred to all things, it certainly is the part of a Christian man to ascend higher than merely to seek and secure the salvation of his own soul. I am persuaded, therefore, that there is no man imbued with true piety, who will not consider as insipid that long and labored exhortation to zeal for heavenly life, a zeal which keeps a man entirely devoted to himself, and does not, even by one expression, arouse him to sanctify the name of God. But I readily agree with you that, after this sanctification, we ought not to propose to ourselves any other object in life than to hasten towards that high calling; for God has set it before us as the constant aim of all our thoughts and words and actions. And, indeed, there is nothing in which man excels the lower animals unless it be his spiritual communion with God in the hope of a blessed eternity. And generally, all we aim at in our discourses is to arouse men to meditate upon it and aspire to it.

I have also no difficulty in conceding to you that there is nothing more perilous to our salvation than a preposterous and perverse worship of God. The primary rudiments by which we are wont to train to piety those whom we wish to gain as disciples to Christ are these; viz., not to frame any new worship of God for themselves at random, and after their own pleasure, but to know that the only legitimate worship is that which He himself approved from the beginning. For we maintain what the sacred oracle declared, that obedience is more excellent than any sacrifice (1 Sam. xv. 22). In short, we train them by every means to be contented with the one rule of worship which they have received from His mouth, and bid adieu to all fictitious worship.

Therefore, Sadoleto, when you uttered this voluntary confession, you laid the foundation of my defense. For if you admit it to be a fearful destruction to the soul when, by false opinions, divine truth is turned into a lie, it now only remains for us to inquire which of the two parties retains that worship of God which is alone legitimate. In order that you may claim it for your party, you assume that the most certain rule of worship is that which is prescribed by the Church, although, as if we here opposed you, you bring the matter under consideration in the manner which is usually observed in regard to doubtful questions. But, Sadoleto, as I see you toiling in vain, I will relieve you from all trouble on this head. You are mistaken in supposing that we desire to lead away the people from that method of worshipping God which the Catholic Church always observed. You either labor under a delusion as to the term *church*, or, at least, knowingly and willingly give it a gloss. I will immediately show the latter to be the case, though it may also be that you are somewhat in error. First, in defining the term, you omit what would have helped you in no small degree to the right understanding of it. When you describe it as that which in all parts, as well as at the present time in every region of the earth, being united and consenting in Christ, has been always and everywhere directed by the one Spirit of Christ, what comes of the Word of the Lord, that clearest of all marks, and which the Lord himself, in pointing out the Church, so often recommends to us? For seeing how dangerous it would be to boast of the Spirit without the Word, He declared that the Church is indeed governed by the Holy Spirit, but in order that that government might not be vague and unstable, He annexed it to the Word. For this reason Christ exclaims that those who are of God hear the Word of God—that His sheep are those which recognize His voice as that of their Shepherd, and any other voice as that of a stranger (John x. 27). For this reason the Spirit, by the mouth of Paul, declares (Eph. ii. 20) that the Church is built upon the foundation of the Apostles and Prophets. Also, that the Church is made holy to the Lord, by the washing of water in the Word of life. The same thing is declared still more clearly by the mouth of Peter, when he teaches that people are regenerated to God by that incorruptible seed (1 Pet. i. 23). In short, why is the preaching of the gospel so often styled the kingdom of God, but because it is the sceptre by which the heavenly King rules His people?

Nor will you find this in the apostolical writings only, but whenever the prophets foretell the renewal of the Church, or its extension over the whole globe, they always assign the first place to the Word. For they tell that from Jerusalem will issue forth living water which, being divided into four rivers, will inundate the whole earth (Zech. xiv. 8). And what these living waters are they themselves explain when they say, "The law will come forth from Zion, and the word of the Lord from Jerusalem" (Is. ii. 3). Well, then, does Chrysostom admonish us to reject all who, under the pretence of the Spirit, lead us away from the simple doctrine of the gospel—the Spirit having been promised not to reveal a new doctrine, but to impress the truth of the gospel on our minds. And we, in fact, experience in the present day how necessary the admonition was. We are assailed by two sects, which seem to differ most widely from each other. For what similitude is there in appearance between the Pope and the Anabaptists? And yet, that you may see that Satan never transforms himself so cunningly as not in some measure to betray himself, the principle weapon with which they both assail us is the same. For when they boast extravagantly of the Spirit, the tendency certainly is to sink and bury the Word of God, that they may make room for their own falsehoods. And you, Sadoleto, by stumbling on the very threshold, have paid the penalty of that affront which you offered to the Holy Spirit when you separated Him from the Word. For, as if those who seek the way of God were standing where two ways meet and destitute of any certain sign, you are forced to introduce them as hesitating whether it be more expedient to follow the authority of the Church, or to listen to those whom you call the inventors of new dogmas. Had you known, or been unwilling to disguise the fact, that the Spirit goes before the Church, to enlighten her in understanding the Word, while the Word itself is like the Lydian stone, by which she tests all doctrines, would you have taken refuge in that most perplexing and thorny question? Learn, then, by your own experience, that it is no less unreasonable to boast of the Spirit without the Word than it would be absurd to bring forward the Word itself without the Spirit. Now, if you can bear to receive a truer definition of the Church than your own, say, in future, that it is the society of all the saints, a society which, spread over the whole world, and existing in all ages, yet bound together by the one doctrine and the one Spirit of Christ, cultivates and observes unity of faith and brotherly concord. With this Church we deny that we have any disagreement. Nay, rather, as we revere her as our mother, so we desire to remain in her bosom.

But here you bring a charge against us. For you teach that all which has been approved for fifteen hundred years or more, by the uniform consent of the faithful, is, by our headstrong rashness, torn up and destroyed. Here I will not require you to deal truly and candidly by us (though this should be spontaneously offered by a philosopher, not to say a Christian). I will only ask you not to stoop to an illiberal indulgence in calumny, which, even though we be silent, must be extremely injurious to your reputation with grave and honest men. You know, Sadoleto, and if you venture to deny, I will make it palpable to all that you knew, yet cunningly and craftily disguised the fact, not only that our agreement with antiquity is far closer that yours, but that all we have attempted has been to renew that ancient form of the Church, which, at first sullied and distorted by illiterate men of indifferent character, was afterward flagitiously mangled and almost destroyed by the Roman Pontiff and his faction.

I will not press you so closely as to call you back to that form which the Apostles instituted (though in it we have the only model of a true Church, and whosoever deviates from it in the smallest degree is in error), but to indulge you so far, place, I pray, before your eyes, that ancient form of the Church, such as their writings prove it to have been in the age of Chrysostom and Basil, among the Greeks, and of Cyprian, Ambrose, and Augustine, among the Latins; after so doing, contemplate the ruins of that Church, as now surviving among yourselves. Assuredly, the difference will appear as great as that which the Prophets describe between the famous Church which flourished under David and Solomon, and that which under Zedekiah and Jehoiakim had lapsed into every kind of superstition, and utterly vitiated the purity of divine worship. Will you here give the name of an enemy of antiquity to him who, zealous for ancient piety and holiness, and dissatisfied with the state of matters as existing in a dissolute and depraved Church, attempts to ameliorate its condition, and restore it to pristine splendor?

Since there are three things on which the safety of the Church is founded, viz., doctrine, discipline, and the sacraments, and to these a fourth is added, viz., ceremonies, by which to exercise the people in offices of piety, in order that we may be most sparing of the honor of your Church, by which of these things would you have us to judge her? The truth of prophetical and evangelical doctrine, on which the Church ought to be founded, has not only in a great measure perished in your Church, but is violently driven away by fire and sword. Will you obtrude upon me, for the Church, a body which furiously persecutes everything sanctioned by our religion, both as delivered by the oracles of God, and embodied in the writings of holy Fathers, and approved by ancient Councils? Where, pray, exist among you any vestiges of that true and holy discipline which the ancient bishops exercised in the Church? Have you not scorned all their institutions? Have you not trampled all the canons under foot? Then, your nefarious profanation of the sacraments I cannot think of without the utmost horror.

Of ceremonies, indeed, you have more than enough, but for the most part so childish in their import, and vitiated by innumerable forms of superstition, as to be utterly unavailing for the preservation of the Church. None of these things, you must be aware, is exaggerated by me in a captious spirit. They all appear so openly that they may be pointed out with the finger wherever there are eyes to behold them. Now, if you please, test us in the same way. You will, assuredly, fall far short of making good the charges which you have brought against us.

In the sacraments, all we have attempted is to restore the native purity from which they had degenerated, and so enable them to resume their dignity. Ceremonies we have in a great measure abolished, but we were compelled to do so; partly because by their multitude they had degenerated into a kind of Judaism, partly because they had filled the minds of the people with superstition, and could not possibly remain without doing the greatest injury to the piety which it was their office to promote. Still we have retained those which seemed sufficient for the circumstances of the times.

That our discipline is not such as the ancient Church professed we do not deny. But with what fairness is a charge of subverting discipline brought against us by those who themselves have utterly abolished it, and in our attempts to reinstate it in its rights have hitherto opposed us? As to our doctrine, we hesitate not to appeal to the ancient Church. And since, for the sake of example, you have touched on certain heads, as to which you thought had some ground for accusing us, I will briefly show how unfairly and falsely you allege that these are things which have been devised by us against the opinion of the Church.

Before descending to particulars, however, I have already cautioned you, and would have you again and again consider with what reason you can charge it upon our people, as a fault, that they have studied to explain the Scriptures. For you are aware that by this study they have thrown such light on the Word of God, that, in this respect, even Envy herself is ashamed to defraud them of all praise. You are just as uncandid when you aver that we have seduced the people by thorny and subtle questions, and so enticed them by that philosophy of which Paul bids Christians beware. What? Do you remember what kind of time it was when our [reformers] appeared, and what kind of doctrine candidates for the ministry learned in the schools? You yourself know that it was mere sophistry, and sophistry so twisted, involved, tortuous, and puzzling, that scholastic theology might well be described as a species of secret magic. The denser the darkness in which any one shrouded a subject, the more he puzzled himself and others with preposterous riddles, the greater his fame for acumen and learning. And when those who had been formed in that forge wished to carry the fruit of their learning to the people, with what skill, I ask, did they edify the Church?

Not to go over every point, what sermons in Europe then exhibited that simplicity with which Paul wishes a Christian people to be always occupied? Nay, what one sermon was there from which old wives might not carry off more whimsies than they could devise at their own fireside in a month? For as sermons were then usually divided, the first half was devoted to those misty questions of the schools which might astonish the rude populace, while the second contained sweet stories, or not unamusing speculations, by which the hearers might be kept on the alert. Only a few expressions were thrown in from the Word of God, that by their majesty they might procure credit for these frivolities. But as soon as our [reformers] raised the standard, all these absurdities, in one moment, disappeared from amongst us. Your preachers, again, partly profited by our books, and partly compelled by shame and the general murmur, conformed to our example, though they still, with open throat, exhale the old absurdity. Hence, any one who compares our method of procedure with the old method, or with that which is still in repute among you, will perceive that you have done us no small injustice. But had you continued your quotation from Paul a little farther, any boy would easily have perceived that the charge which you bring against us is undoubtedly applicable to yourselves. For Paul there interprets "vain philosophy" (Col. ii. 8) to mean that which preys upon pious souls by means of the constitutions of men and the elements of this world: and by these you have ruined the Church.

Even you yourself afterwards acquit us by your own testimony; for among those of our doctrines which you have thought proper to assail, you do not adduce one, the knowledge of which is not essentially necessary for the edification of the Church.

You, in the first place, touch upon justification by faith, the first and keenest subject of controversy between us. Is this a knotty and useless question? Wherever the knowledge of it is taken away, the glory of Christ is extinguished, religion abolished, the Church destroyed, and the hope of salvation utterly overthrown. That doctrine, then, though of the highest moment, we maintain that you have nefariously effaced from the memory of men. Our books are filled with convincing proofs of this fact, and the gross ignorance of this doctrine, which even still continues in all your churches, declares that our complaint is by no means ill-founded. But you very maliciously stir up prejudice against us, alleging that by attributing everything to faith, we leave no room for works.

I will not now enter upon a full discussion, which would require a large volume; but if you would look into the Catechism which I myself drew up for the Genevese, when I held the office of Pastor among them, three words would silence you. Here, however, I will briefly explain to you how we speak on this subject.

First, we bid a man begin by examining himself, and this not in a superficial and perfunctory manner, but to cite his conscience before the tribunal of God, and when sufficiently convinced of his iniquity, to reflect on the strictness of the sentence pronounced upon all sinners. Thus confounded and amazed at his misery, he is prostrated and humbled before God; and, casting away all self-confidence, groans as if given up to final perdition. Then we show that the only haven of safety is in the mercy of God, as manifested in Christ, in whom every part of our salvation is complete. As all mankind are, in the sight of God, lost sinners, we hold that Christ is their only righteousness, since, by His obedience, He has wiped off our transgressions; by His sacrifice, appeased the divine anger; by His blood, washed away our sins; by His cross, borne our curse; and by His death, made satisfaction for us. We maintain that in this way man is reconciled in Christ to God the Father, by no merit of his own, by no value of works, but by gratuitous mercy. When we embrace Christ by faith, and come, as it were, into communion with Him, this we term, after the manner of Scripture, *the righteousness of faith*.

What have you here, Sadoleto, to bite or carp at? Is it that we leave no room for works? Assuredly we do deny that in justifying a man they are worth one single straw. For Scripture everywhere cries aloud, that all are lost; and every man's own conscience bitterly accuses him. The same Scripture teaches that no hope is left but in the mere goodness of God, by which sin is pardoned, and righteousness imputed to us. It declares both to be gratuitous, and finally concludes that a man is justified without works (Rom. iv. 7). But what notion, you ask, does the very term *righteousness* suggest to us if respect is not paid to good works? I answer, if you would attend to the true meaning of the term *justifying* in Scripture, you would have no difficulty. For it does not refer to a man's own righteousness, but to the mercy of God, which contrary to the sinner's deserts, accepts of a righteousness for him, and that by not imputing his unrighteousness. Our righteousness, I say, is that which is described by Paul (2 Cor. v. 19) that God hath reconciled us to Himself in Jesus Christ. The mode is afterwards subjoined—by not imputing sin. He demonstrates that it is by faith only we become partakers of that blessing, when he says that the ministry of reconciliation is contained in the gospel. But faith, you say, is a general term, and has a larger signification. I answer that Paul, whenever he attributes to it the power of justifying, at the same time restricts it to a gratuitous promise of the divine favor, and keeps it far removed from all respect to works. Hence his familiar inference

—if by faith, then not by works. On the other hand—if by works, then not by faith.

But, it seems, injury is done to Christ, if, under the pretence of His grace, good works are repudiated; He having come to prepare a people acceptable to God, zealous of good works, while to the same effect, are many similar passages which prove that Christ came in order that we, doing good works, might, through Him, be accepted by God. This calumny, which our opponents have ever in their mouths, viz., that we take away the desire of well-doing from the Christian life by recommending gratuitous righteousness, is too frivolous to give us much concern. We deny that good works have any share in justification, but we claim full authority for them in the lives of the righteous. For if he who has obtained justification possesses Christ, and at the same time, Christ never is where His Spirit is not, it is obvious that gratuitous righteousness is necssarily connected with regeneration. Therefore, if you would duly understand how inseparable faith and works are, look to Christ, who, as the Apostle teaches (1 Cor. i. 30) has been given to us for justification and for sanctification. Wherever, therefore, that righteousness of faith, which we maintain to be gratuitous, is, there too Christ is, and where Christ is, there too is the Spirit of holiness, who regenerates the soul to newness of life. On the contrary, where zeal for integrity and holiness is not in vigor, there neither is the Spirit of Christ nor Christ Himself; and wherever Christ is not, there is no righteousness, nay, there is no faith; for faith cannot apprehend Christ for righteousness without the Spirit of sanctification.

Since, therefore, according to us, Christ regenerates to a blessed life those whom He justifies, and after rescuing them from the dominion of sin, hands them over to the dominion of righteousness, transforms them into the image of God, and so trains them by His Spirit into obedience to His will, there is no ground to complain that, by our doctrine, lust is left with loosened reins. The passages which you adduce have not a meaning at variance with our doctrine. But if you will pervert them in assailing gratuitous justification, see how unskillfully you argue. Paul elsewhere says (Eph. i. 4) that we were chosen in Christ, before the creation of the world, to be holy and unblameable in the sight of God through love. Who will venture thence to infer either that election is not gratuitous, or that our love is its cause? Nay, rather, as the end of gratuitous election, so also that of gratuitous justification is, that we may lead pure and unpolluted lives before God. For the saying of Paul is true (1 Thess. iv. 7) we have not been called to impurity, but to holiness. This, meanwhile, we constantly maintain, that man is not only justified freely once for all, without any merit of works, but that on this gratuitous justification the salvation of man perpetually depends. Nor is it possible that any work of man can be accepted by God unless it be gratuitously approved. Wherefore, I was amazed when I read your assertion, that love is the first and chief cause of our salvation. O, Sadoleto, who could ever have expected such a saying from you? Undoubtedly the very blind, while in darkness, feel the mercy of God too surely to dare to claim for their love the first cause of their salvation, while those who have merely one spark of divine light feel that their salvation consists in nothing else than their being adopted by God. For eternal salvation is the inheritance of the heavenly Father, and has been prepared solely for His children. Moreover, who can assign any other cause of our adoption than that which is uniformly announced in Scripture, viz., that we did not first love Him, but were spontaneously received by Him into favor and affection?

Your ignorance of this doctrine leads you on to the error of teaching that sins are expiated by penances and satisfactions. Where, then, will be that one expiatory victim, from which, if we depart, there remains, as Scripture testifies, no more sacrifice for sin? Search through all the divine oracles which we possess; if the blood of Christ alone is uniformly set forth as purchasing satisfaction, reconciliation, and ablution, how dare you presume to transfer so great an honor to your works? Nor have you any ground for ascribing this blasphemy to the Church of God. The ancient Church, I admit, had its satisfactions, not those, however, by which sinners might atone to God and ransom themselves from guilt, but by which they might prove that the repentance which they professed was not feigned, and efface the remembrance of that scandal which their sin had occasioned. For satisfactions were not regularly prescribed to all and sundry, but to those only who had fallen into some heinous wickedness.

In the case of the Eucharist, you blame us for attempting to confine the Lord of the universe, and His divine and spiritual power (which is perfectly free and infinite) within the corners of a corporeal nature with its circumscribed boundaries. What end, pray, will there be to calumny? We have always distinctly testified, that not only the divine power of Christ, but His essence also, is diffused over all, and defined by no limits, and yet you hesitate not to upbraid us with confining it within the corners of corporeal nature! How so? Because we are unwilling with you to chain down His body to earthly elements. But had you any regard for sincerity, assuredly you are not ignorant how great a difference there is between the two things—between removing the local presence of Christ's body from bread, and circumscribing His spiritual power within bodily limits. Nor ought you to charge our doctrine with novelty, since it was always held by the Church as an acknowledged point. But as this subject alone would extend to a volume, in order that both of us may escape so toilsome a discussion, the better course will be for you to read Augustine's Epistle to Dardanus, where you will find how one and the same Christ more than fills heaven and earth with the vastness of His divinity, and yet is not everywhere diffused in respect of His humanity.

We loudly proclaim the communion of flesh and blood,

which is exhibited to believers in the Supper; and we distinctly show that that flesh is truly meat, and that blood truly drink —that the soul, not contented with an imaginary conception, enjoys them in very truth. That presence of Christ, by which we are ingrafted in Him, we by no means exclude from the Supper, nor shroud in darkness, though we hold that there must be no local limitation, that the glorious body of Christ must not be degraded to earthly elements; that there must be no fiction of transubstantiating the bread into Christ, and afterward worshipping it as Christ. We explain the dignity and end of this solemn rite in the loftiest terms which we can employ, and then declare how great the advantages which we derive from it. Almost all these things are neglected by you. For overlooking the divine beneficence which is here bestowed upon us, overlooking the legitimate use of so great a benefit (the topics on which it were becoming most especially to dwell), you count it enough that the people gaze stupidly at the visible sign, without any understanding of the spiritual mystery. In condemning your gross dogma of transubstantiation, and declaring that stupid adoration which detains the minds of men among the elements, and permits them not to rise to Christ, to be perverse and impious, we have not acted without the concurrence of the ancient Church, under whose shadow you endeavor in vain to hide the very vile superstitions to which you are here addicted.

In auricular confession we have disapproved of that law of Innocent, which enjoins every man once a year to pass all his sins in review before his priest. It would be tedious to enumerate all the reasons which induced us to abrogate it. But that the thing was nefarious is apparent even from this, that pious consciences, which formerly boiled with perpetual anxiety, have at length begun, after being freed from that dire torment, to rest with confidence in the divine favor; to say nothing, meanwhile, of the many disasters which it brought upon the Church, and which justly entitle us to hold it in execration. For the present, take this for our answer, that it was neither commanded by Christ, nor practiced by the ancient Church. We have forcibly wrested from the hands of the sophists all the passages of Scripture which they had contrived to distort in support of it, while the common books on ecclesiastical history show that it had no existence in an earlier age. The testimonies of the Fathers are to the same effect. It is, therefore, mere deception when you say that the humility therein manifested was enjoined and instituted by Christ and the Church. For though there appears in it a certain show of humility, it is very far from being true that every kind of abasement, which assumes the name of humility, is commended by God. Accordingly, Paul teaches (Col. ii. 18) that that humility only is genuine which is framed in conformity to the Word of God.

In asserting the intercession of the saints, if all you mean is that they continually pray for the completion of Christ's kingdom, on which the salvation of all the faithful depends, there is none of us who calls it in question. Accordingly, you have lost your pains in laboring this part so much, but, no doubt, you were unwilling to lose the opportunity of repeating the false asseveration which charges us with thinking that the soul perishes with the body. That philosophy we leave to your Popes and College of Cardinals, by whom it was for many years most faithfully cultivated, and ceases not to be cultivated in the present day. To them also your subsequent remark applies, viz., to live luxuriously, without any solicitude concerning a future life, and hold us miserable wretches in derision, for laboring so anxiously in behalf of the kingdom of Christ. But in regard to the intercession of the saints, we insist on a point which it is not strange that you omit. For here innumerable superstitions were to be cut off, superstitions which had risen to such a height that the intercession of Christ was utterly erased from men's thoughts, saints were invoked as gods, the peculiar offices of Deity were distributed among them, and a worship paid to them which differed in nothing from that ancient idolatry which we all deservedly execrate.

As to purgatory, we know that ancient churches made some mention of the dead in their prayers, but it was done seldom and soberly, and consisted only of a few words. It was, in short, a mention in which it was obvious that nothing more was meant than to attest in passing the affection which was felt toward the dead. As yet the architects were unborn by whom your purgatory was built, and who afterwards enlarged it to such a width, and raised it to such a height, that it now forms the chief prop of your kingdom. You yourself know what a hydra of errors thence emerged; you know what tricks superstition has at its own hand devised, wherewith to disport itself; you know how many impostures avarice has here fabricated, in order to milk men of every class; you know how great detriment it has done to piety. For not to mention how much true worship has in consequence decayed, the worst result certainly was that while all, without any command from God, were vying with each other in helping the dead, they utterly neglected the congenial offices of charity, which are so strongly enjoined.

I will not permit you, Sadoleto, by inscribing the name of Church on such abominations, both to defame her against all law and justice, and prejudice the ignorant against us, as if we were determined to wage war with the Church. For though we admit that in ancient times some seeds of superstition were sown, which detracted somewhat from the purity of the gospel, still you know that it is not so long ago since those monsters of impiety with which we war were born, or, at least, grew to such a size. Indeed, in attacking, breaking down, and destroying your kingdom, we are armed not only with the energy of the Divine Word, but with the aid of the holy Fathers also.

That I may altogether disarm you of the authority of the Church, which, as your shield of Ajax, you ever and anon oppose to us, I will show, by some additional examples, how widely you differ from that holy antiquity.

We accuse you of overthrowing the ministry, of which the empty name remains with you without the reality. As far as the office of feeding the people is concerned, the very children perceive that bishops and priests are dumb statues, while men of all ranks know by experience that they are active only in robbing and devouring. We are indignant that in the room of the sacred Supper has been substituted a sacrifice, by which the death of Christ is emptied of its virtues. We exclaim against the execrable traffic in masses, and we complain that the Supper of the Lord, as to one of its halves, has been stolen from the Christian people. We inveigh against the accursed worship of images. We show that the sacraments are vitiated by many profane notions. We tell how indulgences crept in with fearful dishonor to the cross of Christ. We lament that, by means of human traditions, Christian liberty has been crushed and destroyed. Of these and similar pests, we have been careful to purge the churches which the Lord has committed to us. Expostulate with us, if you can, for the injury which we inflicted on the Catholic Church, by daring to violate its sacred sanctions. The fact is now too notorious for you to gain anything by denying it, viz., that in all these points, the ancient Church is clearly on our side, and opposes you, not less than we ourselves do.

But here we are met by what you say, when, in order to palliate matters, you allege that though your manners should be irregular, that is no reason why we should make a schism in the holy Church. It is scarcely possible that the minds of the common people should not be greatly alienated from you by the many examples of cruelty, avarice, intemperance, arrogance, insolence, lust, and all sorts of wickedness, which are openly manifested by men of your order, but none of those things would have driven us to the attempt which we made under a much stronger necessity. That necessity was that the light of divine truth had been extinguished, the Word of God buried, the virtue of Christ left in profound oblivion, and the pastoral office subverted. Meanwhile, impiety so stalked abroad that almost no doctrine of religion was pure from admixture, no ceremony free from error, no part, however minute, of divine worship untarnished by superstition. Do those who contend against such evils declare war against the Church, and not rather assist her in her extreme distress? And yet you would take credit for your obedience and humility in refraining, through veneration for the Church, from applying your hand to the removal of these abominations. What has a Christian man to do with that prevaricating obedience, which, while the Word of God is licentiously contemned, yields its homage to human vanity? What has he to do with that contumacious and rude humility, which despising the majesty of God, only looks up with reverence to men? Have done with empty names of virtue, employed merely as cloaks for vice, and let us exhibit the thing itself in its true colors. Ours be the humility which, beginning with the lowest, and paying respect to each in his degree, yields the highest honor and respect to the Church, in subordination, however, to Christ the Church's head; ours the obedience which, while it disposes us to listen to our elders and superiors, tests all obedience by the Word of God; in fine, ours the Church whose supreme care it is humbly and religiously to venerate the Word of God, and submit to its authority.

But what arrogance, you will say, to boast that the Church is with you alone, and to deny it to all the world besides! We indeed, Sadoleto, deny not that those over which you preside are Churches of Christ, but we maintain that the Roman Pontiff, with his whole herd of pseudo-bishops, who have seized upon the pastor's office, are ravening wolves, whose only study has hitherto been to scatter and trample upon the kingdom of Christ, filling it with ruin and devastation. Nor are we the first to make the complaint. With what vehemence does Bernard thunder against Eugenius and all the bishops of his own age? Yet how much more tolerable was its condition then than now? For iniquity has reached its height, and now those shadowy prelates, by whom you think the Church stands or perishes, and by whom we say that she has been cruelly torn and mutilated, and brought to the very brink of destruction, can bear neither their vices nor the cure of them. Destroyed the Church would have been, had not God, with singular goodness, prevented. For in all places where the tyranny of the Roman Pontiff prevails, you scarcely see as many stray and tattered vestiges as will enable you to perceive that there Churches lie half buried. Nor should you think this absurd, since Paul tells you (2 Thess. ii. 4) that Antichrist would have his seat in no other place than in the midst of God's sanctuary. Ought not this single warning to put us on our guard against tricks and devices which may be practiced in the name of the Church?

But whatever the character of the men, still you say it is written, "What they tell you, do." No doubt, if they sit in the chair of Moses. But when from the chair of verity, they intoxicate the people with folly, it is written, "Beware of the leaven of the Pharisees", (Matt. xvi. 6). It is not ours, Sadoleto, to rob the Church of any right which the goodness of God not only has conceded to her, but strictly guarded for her by numerous prohibitions. For as pastors are not sent forth by Him to rule the Church with a licentious and lawless authority, but are astricted to a certain rule of duty which they must not exceed, so the Church is ordered (1 Thess. v. 21; 1 John iv. 1) to see that those who are appointed over her on these terms faithfully accord with their vocation. But we must either hold the testimony of Christ of little moment, or must hold it impious to infringe in the least degree on the authority of those whom He has invested with such splendid titles! Nay, it is you who are mistaken in supposing that the Lord set tyrants over his people to rule them at pleasure, when

He bestowed so much authority on those whom He sent to promulgate the gospel. Your error lies here, viz., in not reflecting that their power, before they were furnished with it, was circumscribed within certain limits. We admit, therefore, that ecclesiastical pastors are to be heard just like Christ Himself, but they must be pastors who execute the office entrusted to them. And this office, we maintain, is not presumptuously to introduce whatever their own pleasure has rashly devised, but religiously and in good faith to deliver the oracles which they have received at the mouth of the Lord. For within these boundaries Christ confined the reverence which He required to be paid to the Apostles; nor does Peter (1 Pet. iv. 11) either claim for himself or allow to others anything more than that, as often as they speak among the faithful, they speak as from the mouth of the Lord. Paul, indeed, justly extols (2 Cor. xiii. 10) the spiritual power with which he was invested, but with this proviso, that it was to avail only for edification, was to wear no semblance of domination, was not to be employed in subjugating faith.

Let your Pontiff, then, boast as he may of the succession of Peter: even should he make good his title to it, he will establish nothing more than that obedience is due to him from the Christian people, so long as he himself maintains his fidelity to Christ, and deviates not from the purity of the gospel. For the Church of the faithful does not force you into any other order than that in which the Lord wished you to stand, when it tests you by that rule by which all your power is defined—the order, I say, which the Lord himself instituted among the faithful, viz., that a Prophet holding the place of teacher should be judged by the congregation (1 Cor. xiv. 29). Whoever exempts himself from this must first expunge his name from the list of Prophets. And here a very wide field for exposing your ignorance opens upon me, since, in matters of religious controversy, all that you leave to the faithful is to shut their own eyes, and to submit implicitly to their teachers.

But since it is certain that every soul which depends not on God alone is enslaved to Satan, how miserable must they be who are imbued with such rudiments of faith? Hence, I observe, Sadoleto, that you have too indolent a theology, as is almost always the case with those who have never had experience in serious struggles of conscience. For otherwise, you would never place a Christian man on ground so slippery, nay, so precipitous, that he can scarcely stand a moment if even the slightest push is given him. Give me, I say, not some unlearned man from among the people, but the rudest clown, and if he is to belong to the flock of God, he must be prepared for that warfare which He has ordained for all the godly. An armed enemy is at hand, on the alert to engage— an enemy most skillful and unassailable by mortal strength; to resist him, with what guards must not that poor man be defended, with what weapons armed, if he is not to be instantly annihilated? Paul informs us (Eph. vi. 17) that the only sword with which he can fight is the Word of the Lord. A soul, therefore, when deprived of the Word of God, is given up unarmed to the devil for destruction. Now, then, will not the first machination of the enemy be to wrest the sword from the soldier of Christ? And what the method of wresting it, but to set him adoubting whether it be the Word of the Lord that he is leaning upon, or the word of man? What will you do for this unhappy being? Will you bid him look round for learned men on whom reclining he may take his rest? But the enemy will not leave him so much as a breathing time in this subterfuge. For when once he has driven him to lean upon men, he will keep urging and repeating his blows until he throws him over the precipice. Thus he must either be easily everthrown, or he must forsake man, and look directly to God. So true it is that Christian faith must not be founded on human testimony, not propped up by doubtful opinion, not reclined on human authority, but engraven on our hearts by the finger of the living God, so as not to be obliterated by any coloring of error. There is nothing of Christ, then, in him who does not hold the elementary principle, that it is God alone who enlightens our minds to perceive His truth, who by His Spirit seals it on our hearts, and by His sure attestation to it confirms our conscience. This is, if I may so express it, that full and firm assurance commended by Paul, and which, as it leaves no room for doubt, so not only does it not hesitate and waver among human arguments as to which party it ought to adhere, but maintains its consistency though the whole world should oppose.

Hence arises that power of judging which we attribute to the Church, and wish to preserve unimpaired. For how much soever the world may fluctuate and jar with contending opinions, the faithful soul is never so destitute as not to have a straight course to salvation. I do not, however, dream of a perspicacity of faith which never errs in discriminating between truth and falsehood, is never deceived; nor do I figure to myself an arrogance which looks down as from a height on the whole human race, waits for no man's judgment, and makes no distinction between learned and unlearned. On the contrary, I admit that pious and truly religious minds do not always attain to all the mysteries of God, but are sometimes blind in the clearest matters—the Lord, doubtless, so providing in order to accustom them to modesty and submission. Again, I admit that they have such a respect for all good men, not to say the Church, that they do not easily allow themselves to be separated from any man in whom they have discovered a true knowledge of Christ; so that sometimes they choose rather to suspend their judgment than to rush, on slight grounds, into dissent. I only contend that so long as they insist on the Word of the Lord, they are never so caught as to be led away to destruction, while their conviction of the truth of the Word of God is so clear and certain that it cannot be overthrown by either men or angels. Away, then, with that nugatory simplicity (which you say becomes the rude and illiterate) of looking up and yielding to the beck of those who are more learned! For besides that the name of faith is undeservedly bestowed on any religious persuasion, however obstinate, which rests anywhere but in God, who can give such a name to some (I know not what) wavering opinion, which is not only easily wrested from them by the arts of the Devil, but fluctuates of its own accord with the temper of the times, and of which no other end can be hoped for than that it will at length vanish away?

As to your assertion that our only aim in shaking off this tyrannical yoke was to set ourselves free for unbridled licentiousness after (so help us!) casting away all thoughts of future life, let judgment be given after comparing our conduct with yours. We abound, indeed, in numerous faults; too often do we sin and fall; still, though truth would, modesty will not, permit me to boast how far we excel you in every respect, unless, perchance, you are to except Rome, that famous abode of sanctity, which having burst asunder the cords of pure discipline, and trodden all honor under foot, has so overflowed with all kinds of iniquity, that scarcely anything so abominable has ever been before. We behooved, forsooth, to expose our heads to so many perils and dangers that we might not, after her example, be placed under too severe constraint! But we have not the least objection that the discipline which was sanctioned by ancient canons should be in force in the present day, and be carefully and faithfully observed; nay, we have always protested that the miserable condition into which the Church had fallen was owing to nothing more than to its enervation by luxury and indulgence. For the body of the Church, to cohere well, must be bound together by discipline as with sinews. But how, on your part, is discipline either observed or desired? Where are those ancient canons with which, like a bridle, bishops and priests were kept to their duty? How are your bishops elected? after what trial? what examination? what care? what caution? How are they inducted to their

office? with what order? what solemnity? They merely take an
official oath that they will perform the pastoral office, and this
apparently for no other end than that they may add perjury
to their other iniquities. Since, then, in seizing upon ecclesiastical offices they seem to enter upon an authority
astricted by no law, they think themselves free to do as they
please, and hence it is that among pirates and robbers there is
apparently more justice and regular government, more effect
given to law, than by all your order.

But since, toward the end, a person has been introduced to
plead our cause, and you have cited us as defenders to the
tribunal of God, I have no hesitation in calling upon you there
to meet me. For such is our consciousness of the truth of our
doctrine, that it has no dread of the heavenly Judge, from
whom, we doubt not, that it proceeded. But it dwells not on
those frivolities with which it has pleased you to amuse yourself; certainly very much out of place. For what more unseason-
able than, after you had come into the presence of God, to set
about devising I know not what follies, and framing for us an
absurd defense which must instantly fail. In pious minds, as
often as that day is suggested, the impression made is too
solemn to leave them at leisure so to disport themselves.
Therefore, frivolity aside, let us think of that day in ex-
pectation of which the minds of men ought ever to be on the
watch. And let us remember that while it is a day to be desired
by the faithful, it is also one at which the ungodly and profane, and those who are despisers of God, may well be
alarmed. Let us turn our ears to the clang of that trumpet
which even the ashes of the dead shall hear in their tombs. Let
us direct our thoughts and minds to that Judge who, by the
mere brightness of His countenance, will disclose whatever
lurks in darkness, lay open all the secrets of the human heart,
and crush all the wicked by the mere breath of His mouth.
Consider, now, what serious answer you are to make for yourself and your party. Our cause, as it is supported by the truth

of God, will be at no loss for a complete defense. I speak not of our persons, whose safety will be found not in defense, but in humble confession and suppliant deprecation, but in so far as our ministry is concerned, there is none of us who will not be able thus to speak:

"O Lord, I have, indeed, experienced how difficult and grievous it was to bear the invidious accusations with which I was harassed on the earth; but with the same confidence with which I then appealed to thy tribunal, I now appear before Thee, because I know that in thy judgment truth always reigns—that truth by whose assurance supported I first ventured to attempt—with whose assistance provided I was able to accomplish whatever I have achieved in thy Church. They charged me with two of the worst of crimes—heresy and schism. And the heresy was that I dared to protest against dogmas which they received. But what could I have done? I heard from thy mouth that there was no other light of truth which could direct our souls into the way of life, than that which was kindled by thy Word. I heard that whatever human minds of themselves conceive concerning thy Majesty, the worship of thy Deity, and the mysteries of thy religion, was vanity. I heard that their introducing into the Church instead of thy Word, doctrines sprung from the human brain, was sacrilegious presumption. But when I turned my eyes towards men, I saw different principles prevailing. Those who were regarded as the leaders of faith neither understood thy Word, nor greatly cared for it. They only drove unhappy people to and fro with strange doctrines, and deluded them with I know not what follies. Among the people themselves, the highest veneration paid to thy Word was to revere it at a distance, as a thing inaccessible, and abstain from all investigation of it. Owing to this supine state of the pastors, and this stupidity of the people, every place was filled with pernicious errors, falsehoods, and superstition. They, indeed, called Thee the only God, but it was while transferring to others the glory which Thou hast claimed for thy Majesty. They figured and had for themselves as many gods as they had saints, whom they chose to worship. Thy Christ was indeed worshipped as God, and retained the name of Saviour; but where He ought to have been honored, He was left almost without honor. For, spoiled of His own virtue, He passed unnoticed among the crowd of saints, like one of the meanest of them. There was none who duly considered that one sacrifice which He offered on the cross, and by which He reconciled us to Thyself—none who ever dreamed of thinking of His eternal priesthood, and the intercession depending upon it—none who trusted in His righteousness only. That confident hope of salvation which is both enjoined by thy Word, and founded upon it, had almost vanished. Nay, it was received as a kind of oracle that it was foolish arrogance, and, as they termed it, presumption for any-one trusting to thy goodness, and the righteousness of thy Son, to entertain a sure and unfaltering hope of salvation. Not a few profane opinions plucked up by the roots the first principles of that doctrine which Thou hast delivered to us in thy Word. The true meaning of Baptism and the Lord's Supper, also, were corrupted by numerous falsehoods. And then, when all, with no small insult to thy mercy, put confidence in good works, when by good works they strove to merit thy favor, to procure justification, to expiate their sins, and make satisfaction to Thee (each of these things obliterating and making void the virtue of Christ's cross), they were yet alto-gether ignorant wherein good works consisted. For just as if they were not at all instructed in righteousness by thy law, they had fabricated for themselves many useless frivolities as a means of procuring thy favor, and on these they so plumed themselves that, in comparison of them, they almost con-temned the standard of true righteousness which thy law recommended—to such a degree had human desires, after usurping the ascendancy, derogated, if not from the belief, at least from the authority, of thy precepts therein contained. That I might perceive these things, Thou, O Lord, didst shine upon me with the brightness of thy Spirit; that I might comprehend how impious and noxious they were, Thou didst bear before me the torch of thy Word; that I might abominate them as they deserved, Thou didst stimulate my soul. But in rendering an account of my doctrine, Thou seest (what my own conscience declares) that it was not my intention to stray beyond those limits which I saw had been fixed by all thy servants. Whatever I felt assured that I had learned from thy mouth, I desired to dispense faithfully to the Church. Assuredly, the thing at which I chiefly aimed, and for which I most diligently labored, was that the glory of thy goodness and justice, after dispersing the mists by which it was formerly obscured, might shine forth conspicuous, that the virtue and blessings of thy Christ (all glosses being wiped away) might be fully displayed. For I thought it impious to leave in obscurity things which we were born to ponder and meditate. Nor did I think that truths, whose magnitude no language can express, were to be maliciously or falsely declared. I hesitated not to dwell at greater length on topics on which the salvation of my hearers depended. For the oracle could never deceive which declares (John. xvii. 3) 'This is eternal life, to know thee the only true God, and Jesus Christ, whom thou has sent.'

"As to the charge of forsaking the Church, which they were wont to bring against me, there is nothing of which my conscience accuses me unless, indeed, he is to be considered a deserter, who, seeing the soldiers routed and scattered, and abandoning the ranks, raises the leader's standard, and recalls them to their posts. For thus, O Lord, were all thy servants dispersed, so that they could not, by any possibility, hear the command, but had almost forgotten their leader, and their service, and their military oath. In order to bring them together when thus scattered, I raised not a foreign standard, but that noble banner of thine whom we must follow, if we would be classed among thy people.

"Then I was assailed by those who, when they ought to have

kept others in their ranks, had led them astray, and when I determined not to desist, opposed me with violence. On this grievous tumults arose, and the contest blazed and issued in disruption. With whom the blame rests it is for Thee, O Lord, to decide. Always, both by word and deed, have I protested how eager I was for unity. Mine, however, was a unity of the Church, which should begin with Thee and end in Thee. For as oft as Thou didst recommend to us peace and concord, Thou, at the same time, didst show that Thou wert the only bond for preserving it. But if I desired to be at peace with those who boasted of being the heads of the Church and pillars of faith, I behooved to purchase it with the denial of thy truth. I thought that anything was to be endured sooner than stoop to such a nefarious paction. For thy Anointed himself hath declared, that though heaven and earth should be confounded, yet thy Word must endure for ever (Matt. xxiv. 35). Nor did I think that I dissented from thy Church, because I was at war with those leaders; for Thou hast forewarned me, both by thy Son and by the apostles, that that place would be occupied by persons to whom I ought by no means to consent. Christ had predicted not of strangers, but of men who should give themselves out for pastors, that they would be ravenous wolves and false prophets, and had, at the same time, cautioned to beware of them. Where Christ ordered me to beware, was I to lend my aid? And the apostles declared that there would be no enemies of thy Church more pestilential than those from within, who should conceal themselves under the title of pastors (Matt. vii. 15; Acts xx. 29; 2 Pet. ii. 1; 1 John ii. 18). Why should I have hesitated to separate myself from persons whom they forewarned me to hold as enemies? I had before my eyes the examples of thy prophets, who I saw had a similar contest with the priests and prophets of their day, though these were undoubtedly the rulers of the Church among the Israelite people. But thy prophets are not regarded as schismatics, because when they wished to revive religion which had fallen into decay, they desisted not, although opposed with utmost violence. They still remained in the unity of the Church, though they were doomed to perdition by wicked priests, and deemed unworthy of a place among men, not to say saints. Confirmed by their example, I too persisted. Though denounced as deserter of the Church, and threatened, I was in no respect deterred, or induced to proceed less firmly and boldly in opposing those who, in the character of pastors, wasted thy Church with a more than impious tyranny. My conscience told me how strong the zeal was with which I burned for the unity of thy Church, provided thy truth were made the bond of concord. As the commotions which followed were not excited by me, so there is no ground for imputing them to me.

"Thou, O Lord, knowest, and the fact itself has testified to men, that the only thing I asked was that all controversies should be decided by thy Word, that thus both parties might unite with one mind to establish thy kingdom; and I declined not to restore peace to the Church at the expense of my head, if I were found to have been unnecessarily the cause of tumult. But what did our opponents? Did they not instantly, and like madmen, fly to fires, swords, and gibbets? Did they not decide that their only security was in arms and cruelty? Did they not instigate all ranks to the same fury? Did they not spurn at all methods of pacification? To this it is owing that a matter, which might at one time have been settled amicably, has blazed into such a contest. But although, amidst the great confusion, the judgments of men were various, I am freed from all fear, now that we stand at thy tribunal, where equity, combined with truth, cannot but decide in favor of innocence."

Such, Sadoleto, is our pleading, not the fictitious one which you, in order to aggravate our case, were pleased to devise, but that the perfect truth of which is known to the good even now, and will be made manifest to all creatures on that day.

Nor will those who, instructed by our preaching, have

adhered to our cause, be at a loss what to say for themselves, since each will be ready with this defense:

"I, O Lord, as I had been educated from a boy, always professed the Christian faith. But at first I had no other reason for my faith than that which then everywhere prevailed. Thy Word, which ought to have shone on all thy people like a lamp, was taken away, or at least suppressed as to us. And lest anyone should long for greater light, an idea had been instilled into the minds of all, that the investigation of that hidden celestial philosophy was better delegated to a few, whom the others might consult as oracles—that the highest knowledge befitting plebeian minds was to subdue themselves into obedience to the Church. Then, the rudiments in which I had been instructed were of a kind which could neither properly train me to the legitimate worship of thy Deity, nor pave the way for me to a sure hope of salvation, nor train me aright for the duties of the Christian life. I had learned, indeed, to worship Thee only as my God, but as the true method of worshipping was altogether unknown to me, I stumbled at the very threshold. I believed, as I had been taught, that I was redeemed by the death of thy Son from liability to eternal death, but the redemption I thought of was one whose virtue could never reach me. I anticipated a future resurrection, but hated to think of it, as being an event most dreadful. And this feeling not only had dominion over me in private, but was derived from the doctrine which was then uniformly delivered to the people by their Christian teachers. They, indeed, preached of thy clemency towards men, but confined it to those who should show themselves deserving of it. They, moreover, placed this desert in the righteousness of works, so that he only was received into thy favor who reconciled himself to Thee by works. Nor, meanwhile, did they disguise the fact, that we are miserable sinners, that we often fall through infirmity of the flesh, and that to all, therefore, thy mercy behooved to be the common haven of salvation; but the method of obtaining it, which they pointed out, was by making satisfaction to Thee for offenses. Then, the satisfaction enjoined was, first, after confessing all our sins to a priest, suppliantly to ask pardon and absolution; and, secondly, by good to efface from thy remembrance our bad actions. Lastly, in order to supply what was still wanting, we were to add sacrifices and solemn expiations. Then, because Thou wert a stern judge and strict avenger of iniquity, they showed how dreadful thy presence must be. Hence they bade us flee first to the saints, that by their intercession Thou mightest be rendered exorable and propitious to us.

"When, however, I had performed all these things, though I had some intervals of quiet, I was still far-off from true peace of conscience; for, whenever I descended into myself, or raised my mind to thee, extreme terror seized me—terror which no expiations nor satisfactions could cure. And the more closely I examined myself, the sharper the stings with which my conscience was pricked, so that the only solace which remained to me was to delude myself by obliviousness. Still, as nothing better offered, I continued the course which I had begun, when, lo, a very different form of doctrine started up, not one which led us away from the Christian profession, but one which brought it back to its fountainhead, and, as it were, clearing away the dross, restored it to its original purity. Offended by the novelty, I lent an unwilling ear, and at first, I confess, strenuously and passionately resisted; for (such is the firmness or effrontery with which it is natural to men to persist in the course which they have once undertaken) it was with the greatest difficulty I was induced to confess that I had all my life long been in ignorance and error. One thing in particular made me averse to those new teachers, viz., reverence for the Church. But when once I opened my ears, and allowed myself to be taught, I perceived that this fear of derogating from the majesty of the Church was groundless. For they reminded me how great the difference is between schism from the Church, and studying to correct the faults by which the

Church herself was contaminated. They spoke nobly of the Church, and showed the greatest desire to cultivate unity. And lest it should seem they quibbled on the term *church*, they showed it was no new thing for Antichrists to preside there in place of pastors. Of this they produced not a few examples, from which it appeared that they aimed at nothing but the edification of the Church, and in that respect were similarly circumstanced with many of Christ's servants whom we ourselves included in the catalogue of saints. For inveighing more freely against the Roman Pontiff, who was reverenced as the viceregent of Christ, the successor of Peter, and the head of the Church, they excused themselves thus: such titles as those are empty bugbears, by which the eyes of the pious ought not to be so blinded as not to venture to look at them, and sift the reality. It was when the world was plunged in ignorance and sloth, as in a deep sleep, that the Pope had risen to such an eminence; certainly neither appointed head of the Church by the Word of God, nor ordained by a legitimate act of the Church, but of his own accord, self-elected. Moreover, the tyranny which he let loose against the people of God was not to be endured, if we wished to have the kingdom of Christ amongst us in safety.

"And they wanted not most powerful arguments to confirm all their positions. First, they clearly disposed everything that was then commonly adduced to establish the primacy of the Pope. When they had taken away all these props, they also, by the Word of God, tumbled him from his lofty height. On the whole, they made it clear and palpable, to learned and unlearned, that the true order of the Church had then perished —that the keys under which the discipline of the Church is comprehended had been altered very much for the worse—that Christian liberty had fallen—in short, that the kingdom of Christ was prostrated when this primacy was reared up. They told me, moreover, as a means of pricking my conscience, that I could not safely connive at these things as if they concerned me not; that so far art Thou from patronising any voluntary error, that even he who is led astray by mere ignorance does not err with impunity. This they proved by the testimony of thy Son (Matt. xv. 14), 'If the blind lead the blind, both shall fall into the ditch.' My mind being now prepared for serious attention, I at length perceived, as if light had broken in upon me, in what a style of error I had wallowed, and how much pollution and impurity I had thereby contracted. Being exceedingly alarmed at the misery into which I had fallen, and much more at that which threatened me in the view of eternal death, I, as in duty bound, made it my first business to betake myself to thy way, condemning my past life, not without groans and tears. And now, O Lord, what remains to a wretch like me, but instead of defense, earnestly to supplicate Thee not to judge according to its deserts that fearful abandonment of thy Word, from which, in thy wondrous goodness, Thou hast at last delivered me."

Now, Sadoleto, if you please, compare this pleading with that which you have put into the mouth of your plebeian. It will be strange if you hesitate which of the two you ought to prefer. For the safety of that man hangs by a thread whose defense turns wholly on this—that he has constantly adhered to the religion handed down to him from his forefathers. At this rate, Jews and Turks and Saracens would escape the judgment of God. Away, then, with this vain quibbling at a tribunal which will be erected not to approve the authority of man, but to condemn all flesh of vanity and falsehood, and vindicate the truth of God only.

But were I disposed to contend with you in trifles, what picture might I paint, I say not of a Pope, or a Cardinal, or any reverend Prelate whatsoever of your faction (in what colors almost every man of them might, without any great stretch of ingenuity, be exhibited, you well know), but of any, even the most select, among your doctors? For his condemnation, there would, assuredly, be no need either to adduce doubtful conjectures against him, or devise false accusations. He would be burdened heavily enough with such as are

certainly just. But that I may not seem to imitate what I blame
in you, I decline this mode of pleading. I will only exhort
these men to turn for once to themselves, and consider with
what fidelity they feed the Christian people, who cannot have
any other food than the Word of their God. And that they
may not flatter themselves too much, because they now act
their part with great applause, and, for the most part, amid
favorable acclamations, let them remember that they have not
yet come to the conclusion, at which, assuredly, they will not
have a theatre on which to vend their smoke with impunity,
and, by their tricks, ensnare credulous minds, but will stand
or fall by the decision of God himself, whose judgment will
not be regulated by the popular gale, but by His own inflexible
justice; and Who will not only inquire into each man's deeds,
but put to proof the hidden sincerity or iniquity of his heart.
I dare not pronounce on all without exception; and yet, how
many of them feel in their consciences that, in contending
against us, they are hiring out their services to men, rather
than [giving them] to God?

While, throughout your letter, you treat us without mercy,
towards its conclusion, you pour out the venom of your bitterness upon us with open mouth. But though your invectives by
no means hurt us, and have already been partly answered, I
would yet ask, what could make you think of accusing us of
avarice? Think you our [reformers] were so dull as not to
perceive from the very outset that they were entering on a
course most adverse to gain and lucre? And when they charged
you with greediness, did they not see that they were neces-
sarily binding themselves to temperance and frugality, if they
were not to become ridiculous even to children? When they
showed that the method of correcting that greediness was to
disburden pastors of their excessive wealth, in order that they
might be more at liberty to care for the Church, did they not
spontaneously shut against themselves the avenue to wealth?
For what riches now remained to which they might aspire?
What! Would not the shortest road to riches and honors have

been to have transacted with you at the very first, on the terms which were offered? How much would your Pontiff then have paid to many for their silence? How much would he pay for it, even at the present day? If they are actuated in the least degree by avarice, why do they cut off all hope of improving their fortune, and prefer to be thus perpetually wretched, rather than enrich themselves without difficulty, and in a twinkling? But ambition, forsooth, withholds them! What ground you had for this other insinuation I see not, since those who first engaged in this cause could expect nothing else than to be spurned by the whole world, and those who afterward adhered to it exposed themselves knowingly and willingly to endless insults and revilings from every quarter. But where is this fraud and inward malice? No suspicion of such things cleaves to us. Talk of them rather in your sacred Consistory, where they are in operation every day.

As I hasten to a conclusion, I am compelled to pass by your calumny that, leaning entirely to our own judgment, we find not in the whole Church one individual to whom we think deference is due. That it is a calumny I have already sufficiently demonstrated. For although we hold that the Word of God alone lies beyond the sphere of our judgment, and that Fathers and Councils are of authority only in so far as they accord with the rule of the Word, we still give to Councils and Fathers such rank and honor as it is meet for them to hold, under Christ.

But the most serious charge of all is, that we have attempted to dismember the Spouse of Christ. Were that true, both you and the whole world might well regard us as desperate. But I will not admit the charge, unless you can make out that the Spouse of Christ is dismembered by those who desire to present her as a chaste virgin to Christ—who are animated by a degree of holy zeal to preserve her spotless for Christ—who, seeing her polluted by base seducers, recall her to conjugal fidelity— who unhesitatingly wage war against all the adulterers whom they detect laying snares for her chastity. And what but this have we done? Had not your faction of a Church attempted, nay, violated her chastity, by strange doctrines? Had she not been violently prostituted by your numberless superstitions? Had she not been defiled by that vilest species of adultery, the worship of images? And because, forsooth, we did not suffer you so to insult the sacred chamber of Christ, we are said to have lacerated His Spouse. But I tell you that that laceration, of which you falsely accuse us, is witnessed not obscurely among yourselves—a laceration not only of the Church, but of Christ himself, who is there beheld miserably mangled. How can the Church adhere to her Spouse, while she has Him not in safety? For where is the safety of Christ, while the glory of His justice, and holiness, and wisdom, is transferred elsewhere?

But it seems, before we kindled the strife, all was tranquillity and perfect peace! True! among pastors, and also among the people, stupor and sloth had caused that there were almost no controversies respecting religion. But in the schools, how lustily did sophists brawl? You cannot, therefore, take credit for a tranquil kingdom, when there was tranquillity for no other reason than because Christ was silent. I admit that, on the revival of the gospel, great disputes arose where all was quietness before. But that is unjustly imputed to our [reformers], who, during the whole course of their proceedings, desired nothing more than that religion being revived, the Churches, which discord had scattered and dispersed, might be gathered together into true unity. And not to go back upon old transactions, what sacrifices did they, on a late occasion, decline to make, merely that they might procure peace to the Churches?* But all their efforts are rendered vain by your

* It would appear that Calvin refers here to a religious conference held in Frankfurt in February, 1539, prior to a meeting of the imperial Diet, to explore the possibility of compromise and reunion. He attended together with Bucer and Sturm from Strasbourg, and met for the first time Melanchthon, with whom he began a close friendship.

opposition. For while they desire peace, that along with it the kingdom of Christ may flourish, and you, on the other hand, think that all which is gained to Christ is lost to you, it is not strange that you strenuously resist. And you have arts by which you can in one day overturn all that they accomplish for the glory of Christ in many months. I will not overwhelm you with words, because one word will make the matter clear. Our [reformers] offered to render an account of their doctrine. If overcome in argument, they decline not to submit. To whom, then, is it owing that the Church enjoys not perfect peace, and the light of truth? Go now, and charge us as seditious, in not permitting the Church to be quiet!

But (that you might not omit any thing which might tend to prejudice our cause) since, during these few years, many sects have sprung up, you, with your usual candor, lay the blame upon us. See with what fairness, or even with what plausibility! If we deserve hatred on that account, the Christian name also must in times of old have deserved it from the ungodly. Therefore, either cease to molest us on this subject, or openly declare that the Christian religion, which begets so many tumults in the world, ought to be banished from the memory of man! It ought not to hurt our cause in the least that Satan has tried in all ways to impede the work of Christ. It were more to the point to inquire which party has devotedly opposed itself to all the sects which have arisen. It is plain that while you were idle and fast asleep, we alone bore all the brunt.

The Lord grant, Sadoleto, that you and all your party may at length perceive, that the only true bond of ecclesiastical unity would exist if Christ the Lord, who hath reconciled us to God the Father, were to gather us out of our present dispersion into the fellowship of His body, that so, through His one Word and Spirit, we might join together with one heart and one soul.

Strasbourg, September 1, 1539

Appendix
on
The Justification Controversy

I

Calvin on Justification

The following statement and explanation of the doctrine of justification by faith alone is taken from the final edition (1559) of Calvin's *Institutes of the Christian Religion*, Book III, Chapter XI, reprinted with permission from *Calvin: Institutes of the Christian Religion*, ed. John T. McNeill, tr. Ford Lewis Battles (copyright © 1960, W. L. Jenkins. Vols. XX and XXI of *The Library of Christian Classics*. Philadelphia: The Westminster Press, 1960), I, 725-754.

JUSTIFICATION BY FAITH: FIRST THE DEFINITION OF THE WORD AND OF THE MATTER

1. Place and meaning of the doctrine of "justification"

I believe I have already explained above, with sufficient care, how for men cursed under the law there remains, in faith, one sole means of recovering salvation. I believe I have also explained what faith itself is, and those benefits of God which it confers upon man, and the fruits it brings forth in him. Let us sum these up. Christ was given to us by God's generosity, to be grasped and possessed by us in faith. By partaking of him, we principally receive a double grace:

namely, that being reconciled to God through Christ's blamelessness, we may have in heaven instead of a Judge a gracious
Father; and secondly, that sanctified by Christ's spirit we may
cultivate blamelessness and purity of life. Of regeneration,
indeed, the second of these gifts, I have said what seemed
sufficient. The theme of justification was therefore more
lightly touched upon because it was more to the point to understand first how little devoid of good works is the faith, through
which alone we obtain free righteousness by the mercy of God;
and what is the nature of the good works of the saints, with
which part of this question is concerned. Therefore we must
now discuss these matters thoroughly. And we must so discuss
them as to bear in mind that this is the main hinge on which
religion turns, so that we devote the greater attention and care
to it. For unless you first of all grasp what your relationship to
God is, and the nature of his judgment concerning you, you
have neither a foundation on which to establish your salvation
nor one on which to build piety toward God. But the need to
know this will better appear from the knowledge itself.

2. The concept of justification

But that we may not stumble on the very threshold—and
this would happen if we should enter upon a discussion of a
thing unknown—first let us explain what these expressions
mean: that man is justified in God's sight, and that he is
justified by faith or works. He is said to be justified in God's
sight who is both reckoned righteous in God's judgment and
has been accepted on account of his righteousness. Indeed, as
iniquity is abominable to God, so no sinner can find favor
in his eyes in so far as he is a sinner and so long as he is
reckoned as such. Accordingly, wherever there is sin, there
also the wrath and vengeance of God show themselves. Now
he is justified who is reckoned in the condition not of a sinner,
but of a rightous man; and for that reason, he stands firm before God's judgment seat while all sinners fall. If an innocent

accused person be summoned before the judgment seat of a fair judge, where he will be judged according to his innocence, he is said to be "justified" before the judge. Thus, justified before God is the man who, freed from the company of sinners, has God to witness and affirm his righteousness. In the same way, therefore, he in whose life that purity and holiness will be found which deserves a testimony of righteousness before God's throne will be said to be justified by works, or else he who, by the wholeness of his works, can meet and satisfy God's judgment. On the contrary, justified by faith is he who, excluded from the righteousness of works, grasps the righteousness of Christ through faith, and clothed in it, appears in God's sight not as a sinner but as a righteous man.

Therefore, we explain justification simply as the acceptance with which God receives us into his favor as righteous men. And we say that it consists in the remission of sins and the imputation of Christ's righteousness.

3. Scriptural usage

There are many clear testimonies of Scripture to confirm this fact. First, it cannot be denied that this is a proper and most customary meaning of the word. But because it would take too long to collect all the passages and to compare them, let it suffice to have called them to our readers' attention, for they will readily observe such of themselves. I shall bring forward only a few, where this justification of which we are speaking is expressly treated.

First, when Luke relates that the people, having heard Christ, justified God [Luke 7:29], and when Christ declares that "wisdom is justified by . . . her children" [Luke 7:35], Luke in the former passage (v. 29) does not mean that they confer righteousness. For righteousness always remains undivided with God, although the whole world tries to snatch it away from him. Nor does he, in v. 35, intend to justify the doctrine of salvation, which is righteous of itself. Rather, both expressions have the same force—to render to God and his teaching the praise they deserve. On the other hand, when Christ upbraids the Pharisees for justifying themselves [Luke 16:15], he does not mean that they acquire righteousness by well-doing but that they ambitiously seize upon a reputation for righteousness of which they are devoid. Those skilled in the Hebrew language better understand this sense: where not only those who are conscious of their crime but those who undergo the judgment of damnation are called "wicked." For when Bathsheba says that she and Solomon will be wicked [I Kings 1:21], she does not acknowledge any offense. But she complains that she and her son are going to be put to shame, to be counted among the wicked and condemned. Yet from the context it readily appears that this word, even when it is read in Latin, cannot otherwise be understood than relatively, but not so as to signify any quality.

But, because it pertains to the present case, when Paul says that Scripture foresaw that God would justify the Gentiles by faith [Gal. 3:8], what else may you understand but that God imputes righteousness by faith? Again, when he says that God justifies the impious person who has faith in Christ [Rom. 3:26 p.], what can his meaning be except that men are freed by the benefit of faith from that condemnation which their impiety deserved? This appears even more clearly in his conclusion, when he exclaims: "Who will accuse God's elect? It is God who justifies. Who will condemn? It is Christ who died, yes, who rose again . . . and now intercedes for us" [Rom. 8:33–34 p.]. For it is as if he had said: "Who will accuse those whom God has absolved? Who will condemn those whom Christ defends with his protection?" Therefore, "to justify" means nothing else than to acquit of guilt him who was accused, as if his innocence were confirmed. Therefore, since God justifies us by the intercession of Christ, he absolves us not by the confirmation of our own innocence but by the imputation of righteousness, so that we who are not righteous in ourselves may be reckoned as such in Christ. Thus it is said in Paul's sermon in the thirteenth chapter of The Acts: Through Christ is forgiveness of sins announced to you, and everyone who believes in him is justified of all things from which the law of Moses could not justify him [Acts 13:38–39]. You see that, after forgiveness of sins, this justification is set down, as it were, by way of interpretation. You see that it is plainly understood as absolution, you see that it is separated from the works of the law. You see it as the mere benefit of Christ, and you see that it is received by faith. You see finally that a satisfaction is introduced where he says that we are justified from our sins through Christ. Thus, when the publican is said to have gone down from the Temple justified [Luke 18:14], we cannot say that he achieved righteousness by any merit of works. This, therefore, is what is said: after pardon of sins has been obtained, the sinner is considered as a just man in God's sight. Therefore, he was righteous not by approval of works but by God's free absolution. Ambrose has, accordingly, fitly expressed it when he calls the confession of sins a lawful justification.

4. Justification as gracious acceptance by God and as forgiveness of sins

And to avoid contention over a word, if we look upon the thing itself as described to us, no misgiving will remain. For Paul surely refers to justification by the word "acceptance" when in Eph. 1:5–6 he says: "We are destined for adoption through Christ according to God's good pleasure, to the praise of his glorious grace by which he has accounted us acceptable and beloved" [Eph. 1:5–6 p.]. That means the very thing that he commonly says elsewhere, that "God justifies us freely" [Rom. 3:24]. Moreover, in the fourth chapter of Romans he first calls justification "imputation of righteousness." And he does not hesitate to include it within forgiveness of sins. Paul says: "That man is declared blessed by David whom God renders acceptable or to whom he imputes righteousness apart from works, as it is written: 'Blessed are they whose transgressions have been forgiven' " [Rom. 4:6–7 p.; Ps. 32:1]. There he is obviously discussing not a part of justification but the whole of it. Further, he approves the definition of it set forth by David when he declares those men blessed to whom free pardon of sins is given [Ps. 32:1–2]. From this it is clear that the righteousness of which he speaks is simply set in opposition to guilt. But the best passage of all on this matter is the one in which he teaches that the sum of the gospel embassy is to reconcile us to God, since God is willing to receive us into grace through Christ, not counting our sins against us [II Cor. 5:18–20]. Let my readers carefully ponder the whole passage. For a little later Paul adds by way of explanation: "Christ, who was without sin, was made sin for us" [II Cor. 5:21], to designate the means of reconciliation [cf. vs. 18–19]. Doubtless, he means by the word "reconciled" nothing but "justified." And surely, what he teaches elsewhere—that "we are made righteous by Christ's obedience" [Rom. 5:19 p.]—could not stand unless we are reckoned righteous before God in Christ and apart from ourselves.*

13. Righteousness by faith and righteousness by works

But a great part of mankind imagine that righteousness is composed of faith and works. Let us also, to begin with, show that faith righteousness so differs from works righteousness that when one is established the other has to be overthrown. The apostle says that he "counts everything as dross" that he "may gain Christ and be found in him, . . . not having a righteousness of [his] own, based on law, but one that is through faith in Jesus Christ, the righteousness from God through faith" [Phil. 3:8–9 p.]. You see here both a com-

---

* Sections 5 through 12 of this chapter, which have not been reprinted here, discuss and reply to the teaching of Andreas Osiander (1498–1552) regarding justification. Osiander, Lutheran reformer at Nürnberg and later professor at Königsberg, came to hold a doctrine of "essential righteousness" which differed sharply from the Lutheran and Calvinist concept of imputed justification.

parison of opposites and an indication that a man who wishes to obtain Christ's righteousness must abandon his own righteousness. Therefore, he states elsewhere that this was the cause of the Jews' downfall: "Wishing to establish their own righteousness, they did not submit to God's righteousness" [Rom. 10:3 p.]. If by establishing our own righteousness we shake off the righteousness of God, to attain the latter we must indeed completely do away with the former. He also shows this very thing when he states that our boasting is not excluded by law but by faith [Rom. 3:27]. From this it follows that so long as any particle of works righteousness remains some occasion for boasting remains with us. Now, if faith excludes all boasting, works righteousness can in no way be associated with faith righteousness. In this sense he speaks so clearly in the fourth chapter of Romans that no place is left for cavils or shifts: "If Abraham," says Paul, "was justified by works, he has something to boast about." He adds, "Yet he has no reason to boast before God" [Rom. 4:2]. It follows, therefore, that he was not justified by works. Then Paul sets forth another argument from contraries. When reward is made for works it is done out of debt, not of grace [Rom. 4:4]. But righteousness according to grace is owed to faith. Therefore it does not arise from the merits of works. Farewell, then, to the dream of those who think up a righteousness flowing together out of faith and works.

14. Likewise, the works of the regenerated can procure no justification

The Sophists, who make game and sport in their corrupting of Scripture and their empty caviling, think they have a subtle evasion. For they explain "works" as meaning those which men not yet reborn do only according to the letter by the effort of their own free will, apart from Christ's grace. But they deny that these refer to spiritual works. For, according to them, man is justified by both faith and works provided they are not his own works but the gifts of Christ and the fruit of regeneration. For they say that Paul so spoke for no other reason than to convince the Jews, who were relying upon their own strength, that they were foolish to arrogate righteousness to themselves, since the Spirit of Christ alone bestows it upon us not through any effort arising from our own nature. Still they do not observe that in the contrast between the righteousness of the law and of the gospel, which Paul elsewhere introduces, all works are excluded, whatever title may grace them [Gal. 3:11–12]. For he teaches that this is the righteousness of the law, that he who has fulfilled what the law commands should obtain salvation; but this is the righteousness of faith, to believe that Christ died and rose again [Rom. 10:5, 9].

Moreover, we shall see afterward, in its proper place, that the benefits of Christ—sanctification and righteousness—are different. From this it follows that not even spiritual works come into account when the power of justifying is ascribed to faith. The statement of Paul where he denies that Abraham had any reason to boast before God—a passage that we have just cited—because he was not righteous by his works, ought not to be restricted to a literal and outward appearance of virtues or to the effort of free will. But even though the life of the patriarch was spiritual and well-nigh angelic, he did not have sufficient merit of works to acquire righteousness before God.

15. The Roman doctrine of grace and good works

Somewhat too gross are the Schoolmen, who mingle their concoctions. Yet these men infect the simple-minded and unwary with a doctrine no less depraved, cloaking under the disguise of "spirit" and "grace" even the mercy of God, which alone can set fearful souls at rest. Now we confess with Paul that the doers of the law are justified before God; but, because we are all far from observing the law, we infer from this that those works which ought especially to avail for righteousness give us no help because we are destitute of them.

As regards the rank and file of the papists or Schoolmen,

they are doubly deceived here both because they call faith an assurance of conscience in awaiting from God their reward for merits and because they interpret the grace of God not as the imputation of free righteousness but as the Spirit helping in the pursuit of holiness. They read in the apostle: "Whoever would draw near to God must first believe that he exists and then that he rewards those who seek him" [Heb. 11:6]. But they pay no attention to the way in which he is to be sought. It is clear from their own writings that in using the term "grace" they are deluded. For Lombard explains that justification is given to us through Christ in two ways. First, he says, Christ's death justifies us, while love is aroused through it in our hearts and makes us righteous. Second, because through the same love, sin is extinguished by which the devil held us captive, so that he no longer has the wherewithal to condemn us. You see how he views God's grace especially in justification, in so far as we are directed through the grace of the Holy Spirit to good works. Obviously, he intended to follow Augustine's opinion, but he follows it at a distance and even departs considerably from the right imitation of it. For when Augustine says anything clearly, Lombard obscures it, and if there was anything slightly contaminated in Augustine, he corrupts it. The schools have gone continually from bad to worse until, in headlong ruin, they have plunged into a sort of Pelagianism. For that matter, Augustine's view, or at any rate his manner of stating it, we must not entirely accept. For even though he admirably deprives man of all credit for righteousness and transfers it to God's grace, he still subsumes grace under sanctification, by which we are reborn in newness of life through the Spirit.

16. *Our justification according to the judgment of Scripture*

But Scripture, when it speaks of faith righteousness, leads us to something far different: namely, to turn aside from the contemplation of our own works and look solely upon God's mercy and Christ's perfection. Indeed, it presents this order of justification: to begin with, God deigns to embrace the sinner with his pure and freely given goodness, finding nothing in him except his miserable condition to prompt Him to mercy, since he sees man utterly void and bare of good works; and so he seeks in himself the reason to benefit man. Then God touches the sinner with a sense of his goodness in order that he, despairing of his own works, may ground the whole of his salvation in God's mercy. This is the experience of faith through which the sinner comes into possession of his salvation when from the teaching of the gospel he acknowledges that he has been reconciled to God: that with Christ's righteousness interceding and forgiveness of sins accomplished he is justified. And although regenerated by the Spirit of God, he ponders the everlasting righteousness laid up for him not in the good works to which he inclines but in the sole righteousness of Christ. When these things are pondered one by one, they will give a clear explanation of our opinion. However, they might be arranged in another order, better than the one in which they have been set forth. But it makes little difference, provided they so agree among themselves that we may have the whole matter rightly explained and surely confirmed.

17. Faith righteousness and law righteousness according to Paul

Here we should recall to mind the relation that we have previously established between faith and the gospel. For faith is said to justify because it receives and embraces the righteousness offered in the gospel. Moreover, because righteousness is said to be offered through the gospel, all consideration of works is excluded. Paul often shows this elsewhere but most clearly in two passages. For in comparing the law and the gospel in the letter to the Romans he says: "the righteousness that is of the law" is such that "the man who practices these things will live by them" [Rom. 10:5]. But the "righteousness that is of faith" [Rom. 10:6] announces salvation "if you believe in your heart and confess with your mouth that Jesus is Lord and that the Father raised him from the dead" [Rom. 10:9 p.]. Do you see how he makes this the distinction between law and gospel: that the former attributes righteousness to works, the latter bestows free righteousness apart from the help of works? This is an important passage, and one that can extricate us from many difficulties if we understand that that righteousness which is given us through the gospel has been freed of all conditions of the law. Here is the reason why he so often opposes the promise to the law, as things mutually contradictory: "If the inheritance is by the law, it is no longer by promise" [Gal. 3:18]; and passages in the same chapter that express this idea.

Now, to be sure, the law itself has its own promises. Therefore, in the promises of the gospel there must be something distinct and different unless we would admit that the comparison is inept. But what sort of difference will this be, other than that the gospel promises are free and dependent solely upon God's mercy, while the promises of the law depend upon the condition of works? And let no one here snarl at me that it is the righteousness which men, of their own strength and free will, would obtrude upon God that is rejected—inasmuch as Paul unequivocally teaches that the law, in commanding, profits nothing [cf. Rom. 8:3]. For there is no one, not only of the common folk, but of the most perfect persons, who can fulfill it. To be sure, love is the capstone of the law. When the Spirit of God forms us to such love, why is it not for us a cause of righteousness, except that even in the saints it is imperfect, and for that reason merits no reward of itself?

18. *Justification not the wages of works, but a free gift*

The second passage is this: "It is evident that no man is justified before God by the law. For the righteous shall live by faith [cf. Hab. 2:4]. But the law is not of faith;

rather, the man who does these things shall live in them"
[Gal. 3:11–12]. How would this argument be maintained
otherwise than by agreeing that works do not enter the
account of faith but must be utterly separated? The
law, he says, is different from faith. Why? Because works are
required for law righteousness. Therefore it follows that they
are not required for faith righteousness. From this relation it
is clear that those who are justified by faith are justified apart
from the merit of works—in fact, without the merit of works.
For faith receives that righteousness which the gospel bestows.
Now the gospel differs from the law in that it does not link
righteousness to works but lodges it solely in God's mercy.
Paul's contention in Romans is similar to this: that Abraham
had no occasion to boast, for faith was reckoned as righteousness for him [Rom. 4:2–3]; and he adds as confirmation that
the righteousness of faith has a place in circumstances where
there are no works for which a reward is due. "Where," he
says, "there are works, wages are paid as a debt; what is given
to faith is free." [Rom. 4:4–5 p.] Indeed, the meaning of the
words he uses there applies also to this passage. He adds a
little later that we on this account obtain the inheritance from
faith, as according to grace. Hence he infers that this inheritance is free, for it is received by faith [cf. Rom. 4:16].
How is this so except that faith rests entirely upon God's
mercy without the assistance of works? And in another passage he teaches, doubtless in the same sense, that "the righteousness of God has been manifested apart from law, although
it is attested by the Law and the Prophets" [Rom. 3:21 p.].
For, excluding the law, he denies that we are aided by works
and that we attain righteousness by working; instead, we
come empty to receive it.

19. Through "faith alone"

Now the reader sees how fairly the Sophists today cavil
against our doctrine when we say that man is justified by faith

alone [Rom. 3:28]. They dare not deny that man is justified
by faith because it recurs so often in Scripture. But since the
word "alone" is nowhere expressed, they do not allow this
addition to be made. Is it so? But what will they reply to these
words of Paul where he contends that righteousness cannot
be of faith unless it be free [Rom. 4:2 ff.]? How will a free
gift agree with works? With what chicaneries will they elude
what he says in another passage, that God's righteousness is
revealed in the gospel [Rom. 1:17]? If righteousness is revealed in the gospel, surely no mutilated or half righteousness
but a full and perfect righteousness is contained there. The
law therefore has no place in it. Not only by a false but by
an obviously ridiculous shift they insist upon excluding this
adjective. Does not he who takes everything from works firmly
enough ascribe everything to faith alone? What, I pray, do
these expressions mean: "His righteousness has been manifested apart from the law" [Rom. 3:21 p.]; and, "Man is freely
justified" [Rom. 3:24 p.]; and, "Apart from the works of the
law" [Rom. 3:28]?

Here they have an ingenious subterfuge: even though they
have not devised it themselves but have borrowed it from
Origen and certain other ancient writers, it is still utterly
silly. They prate that the ceremonial works of the law are
excluded, not the moral works. They become so proficient by
continual wrangling that they do not even grasp the first
elements of logic. Do they think that the apostle was raving
when he brought forward these passages to prove his opinion?
"The man who does these things will live in them" [Gal.
3:12], and, "Cursed be every one who does not fulfill all
things written in the book of the law" [Gal. 3:10 p.]. Unless
they have gone mad they will not say that life was promised
to keepers of ceremonies or the curse announced only to those
who transgress the ceremonies. If these passages are to be
understood of the moral law, there is no doubt that moral
works are also excluded from the power of justifying. These

arguments which Paul uses look to the same end: "Since through the law comes knowledge of sin" [Rom. 3:20], therefore not righteousness. Because "the law works wrath" [Rom. 4:15], hence not righteousness. Because the law does not make conscience certain, it cannot confer righteousness either. Because faith is imputed as righteousness, righteousness is therefore not the reward of works but is given unearned [Rom. 4:4–5]. Because we are justified by faith, our boasting is cut off [Rom. 3:27 p.]. "If a law had been given that could make alive, then righteousness would indeed be by the law. But God consigned all things to sin that the promise might be given to those who believe." [Gal. 3:21–22 p.] Let them now babble, if they dare, that these statements apply to ceremonies, not to morals. Even schoolboys would hoot at such impudence. Therefore, let us hold as certain that when the ability to justify is denied to the law, these words refer to the whole law.

20. "Works of the law"

If anyone should wonder why the apostle, not content with naming works, uses such a qualification, there is a ready explanation. Though works are highly esteemed, they have their value from God's approval rather than from their own worth. For who would dare recommend works righteousness to God unless God himself approved? Who would dare demand a reward due unless he promised it? Therefore, it is from God's beneficence that they are considered worthy both of the name of righteousness and of the reward thereof. And so, for this one reason, works have value, because through them man intends to show obedience to God. Therefore, to prove that Abraham could not be justified by works, the apostle declares in another place that the law was given fully four hundred and thirty years after the covenant was made [Gal. 3:17]. The ignorant would laugh at this sort of argument, on the ground that before the promulgation of the law there could have been righteous works. But because he knew that works could have such great value only by the testimony and vouchsafing of God, he took as a fact that previous to the law they had no power to justify. We have the reason why he expressly mentions the works of the law when he wants to take justification away from them, for it is clearly because a controversy can be raised only over them.

Yet he sometimes excepts all works without any qualification, as when on David's testimony he states that blessedness is imparted to that man to whom God reckons righteousness apart from works [Rom. 4:6; Ps. 32:1–2]. Therefore no cavils of theirs can prevent us from holding to the exclusive expression as a general principle.

Also, they pointlessly strive after the foolish subtlety that we are justified by faith alone, which acts through love, so that righteousness depends upon love. Indeed, we confess with Paul that no other faith justifies "but faith working through love" [Gal. 5:6]. But it does not take its power to justify from that working of love. Indeed, it justifies in no other way but in that it leads us into fellowship with the righteousness of Christ. Otherwise, everything that the apostle insists upon so vigorously would fall. "Now to him who works the pay is not considered a gift but his due," says he. [Rom. 4:4] "But to one who does not work but believes in him who justifies the ungodly, his faith is reckoned as righteousness." [Rom. 4:5] Could he have spoken more clearly than in contending thus: that there is no righteousness of faith except where there are no works for which a reward is due? And then that faith is reckoned as righteousness only where righteousness is bestowed through a grace not owed?

21. Justification, reconciliation, forgiveness of sins

Now let us examine how true that statement is which is spoken in the definition, that the righteousness of faith is reconciliation with God, which consists solely in the forgiveness of sins. We must always return to this axiom: the wrath of God rests upon all so long as they continue to be sinners. Isaiah has very well expressed it in these words: "The Lord's hand is not shortened, that it cannot save, or his ear dull, that it cannot hear; but your iniquities have made a separation between you and your God, and your sins have hid his face from you lest he hear" [Isa. 59:1–2]. We are told that sin is division between man and God, the turning of God's face away from the sinner; and it cannot happen otherwise, seeing that it is foreign to his righteousness to have any dealings with sin. For this reason, the apostle teaches that man is God's enemy until he is restored to grace through Christ [Rom. 5:8–10]. Thus, him whom he receives into union with himself the Lord is said to justify, because he cannot receive him into grace nor join him to himself unless he turns him from a sinner into a righteous man. We add that this is done through forgiveness of sins; for if those whom the Lord has reconciled to himself be judged by works, they will indeed still be found sinners, though they ought, nevertheless, to be freed and cleansed from sin. It is obvious, therefore, that those whom God embraces are made righteous solely by the fact that they are purified when their spots are washed away by forgiveness of sins. Consequently, such righteousness can be called, in a word, "remission of sins."

22. *Scriptural proof for the close relation between justification and forgiveness of sins*

Paul's words, which I have already quoted, express both of these points very beautifully: "God was in Christ reconciling the world to himself, not counting men's trespasses against them, and has entrusted to us the word of reconciliation" [II Cor. 5:19]. Then Paul adds the summation of Christ's embassy: "Him who knew not sin he made to be sin for us so that we might be made the righteousness of God in him" [II Cor. 5:21]. Here he mentions righteousness and reconciliation indiscriminately, to have us understand that each one is reciprocally contained in the other. Moreover, he teaches the way in which this righteousness is to be obtained: namely, when our sins are not counted against us. Therefore, doubt no longer how God may justify us when you hear that he reconciles us to himself by not counting our sins against us. Thus, by David's testimony Paul proves to the Romans that righteousness is imputed to man apart from works, for David declares that man "blessed whose transgressions are forgiven, whose sins are covered, to whom the Lord has not imputed iniquity" [Rom. 4:6–8; Ps. 32:1–2]. Undoubtedly, he there substitutes blessedness for righteousness; since he declares that it consists in forgiveness of sins, there is no reason to define it differently. Accordingly, Zechariah, the father of John the Baptist, sings that the knowledge of salvation rests in the forgiveness of sins [Luke 1:77]. Paul followed this rule in the sermon on the sum of salvation that he delivered to the people of Antioch. As Luke reports it, he concluded in this way: "Through this man forgiveness of sins is proclaimed to you, and every one that believes in him is justified from all things from which you could not be justified by the law of Moses" [Acts 13:38–39 p.]. The apostle so connects forgiveness of sins with righteousness that he shows them to be exactly the same. From this he duly reasons that the righteousness that we obtain through God's kindness is free to us.

And this ought not to seem an unusual expression, that believers are made righteous before God not by works but by free acceptance, since it occurs so often in Scripture, and ancient writers also sometimes speak thus. So says Augustine in one place: "The righteousness of the saints in this world consists more in the forgiveness of sins than in perfection of virtues." Bernard's famous sentences correspond to this: "Not to sin is the righteousness of God; but the righteousness of man is the grace of God." And he had previously declared: "Christ is our righteousness in absolution, and therefore those alone are righteous who obtain pardon from his mercy."

23. *Righteous—not in ourselves but in Christ*

From this it is also evident that we are justified before God solely by the intercession of Christ's righteousness. This is equivalent to saying that man is not righteous in himself but because the righteousness of Christ is communicated to him by imputation—something worth carefully noting. Indeed, that frivolous notion disappears, that man is justified by faith because by Christ's righteousness he shares the Spirit of God, by whom he is rendered righteous. This is too contrary to the above doctrine ever to be reconciled to it. And there is no doubt that he who is taught to seek righteousness outside himself is destitute of righteousness in himself. Moreover, the apostle most clearly asserts this when he writes: "He who knew not sin was made the atoning sacrifice of sin for us so that we might be made the righteousness of God in him" [II Cor. 5:21 p.].

You see that our righteousness is not in us but in Christ, that we possess it only because we are partakers in Christ; indeed, with him we possess all its riches. And this does not contradict what he teaches elsewhere, that sin has been condemned for sin in Christ's flesh that the righteousness of the law might be fulfilled in us [Rom. 8:3–4]. The only fulfillment he alludes to is that which we obtain through imputation. For in such a way does the Lord Christ share his righteousness with us that, in some wonderful manner, he pours into us enough of his power to meet the judgment of God. It is quite clear that Paul means exactly the same thing in another statement, which he had put a little before: "As we were made sinners by one man's disobedience, so we have been justified by one man's obedience" [Rom. 5:19 p.]. To declare that by him alone we are accounted righteous, what else is this but to lodge our righteousness in Christ's obedience, because the obedience of Christ is reckoned to us as if it were our own?

For this reason, it seems to me that Ambrose beautifully stated an example of this righteousness in the blessing of Jacob: noting that, as he did not of himself deserve the right of the first-born, concealed in his brother's clothing and wearing his brother's coat, which gave out an agreeable odor [Gen. 27:27], he ingratiated himself with his father, so that to his own benefit he received the blessing while impersonating another. And we in like manner hide under the precious purity of our first-born brother, Christ, so that we may be attested righteous in God's sight. Here are the words of Ambrose: "That Isaac smelled the odor of the garments perhaps means that we are justified not by works but by faith, since the weakness of the flesh is a hindrance to works, but the brightness of faith, which merits the pardon of sins, overshadows the error of deeds."

And this is indeed the truth, for in order that we may appear before God's face unto salvation we must smell sweetly with his odor, and our vices must be covered and buried by his perfection.

II

The Council of Trent on Justification

The following document is the decree concerning justification and
the accompanying canons promulgated at the sixth session of the
Council of Trent on January 13, 1547, reprinted with permission
from *Canons and Decrees of the Council of Trent,* tr. H. J.
Schroeder (St. Louis: B. Herder Book Co., 1941), pp. 29-46. For
an evaluation, see Jedin, II 307 ff.

DECREE CONCERNING JUSTIFICATION

INTRODUCTION

Since there is being disseminated at this time, not without
the loss of many souls and grievous detriment to the unity of
the Church, a certain erroneous doctrine concerning justification, the holy, ecumenical and general Council of Trent,
lawfully assembled in the Holy Ghost, the most reverend
John Maria, Bishop of Praeneste de Monte, and Marcellus,
priest of the Holy Cross in Jerusalem, cardinals of the holy
Roman Church and legates Apostolic *a latere,* presiding in
the name of our most holy Father and Lord in Christ, Paul III,
by the providence of God, Pope, intends, for the praise and
glory of Almighty God, for the tranquillity of the Church
and the salvation of souls, to expound to all the faithful of
Christ the true and salutary doctrine of justification, which
the *Sun of justice,*[1] Jesus Christ, *the author and finisher of
our faith*[2] taught, which the Apostles transmitted and which
the Catholic Church under the inspiration of the Holy Ghost
has always retained; strictly forbidding that anyone hence-

[1] Mal. 4:2.
[2] Heb. 12:2.

forth presume to believe, preach or teach otherwise than is defined and declared in the present decree.

CHAPTER I

THE IMPOTENCY OF NATURE AND OF THE LAW TO JUSTIFY MAN

The holy council declares first, that for a correct and clear understanding of the doctrine of justification, it is necessary that each one recognize and confess that since all men had lost innocence in the prevarication of Adam,[3] having become unclean,[4] and, as the Apostle says, *by nature children of wrath,*[5] as has been set forth in the decree on original sin,[6] they were so far *the servants of sin*[7] and under the power of the devil and of death, that not only the Gentiles by the force of nature, but not even the Jews by the very letter of the law of Moses were able to be liberated or to rise therefrom, though free will, weakened as it was in its powers and downward bent,[8] was by no means extinguished in them.

CHAPTER II

THE DISPENSATION AND MYSTERY OF THE ADVENT OF CHRIST

Whence it came to pass that the heavenly Father, *the Father of mercies and the God of all comfort,*[9] when the blessed ful-

[3] Rom. 5:12; I Cor. 15:22.
[4] Is. 64:6.
[5] Eph. 2:3.
[6] Cf. Sess. V.
[7] Rom. 6:17, 20.
[8] Cf. II Synod of Orange (529), c.25. Hardouin, II, 1101.
[9] See II Cor. 1:3.

ness of the time was come,[10] sent to men Jesus Christ, His own
Son, who had both before the law and during the time of the
law been announced and promised to many of the holy
fathers,[11] *that he might redeem the Jews who were under the
law,*[12] and *that the Gentiles who followed not after justice*[13]
might attain to justice, and that all men might receive the
adoption of sons. Him has God *proposed* as a propitiator
through faith in his blood[14] *for our sins, and not for our sins
only, but also for those of the whole world.*[15]

Chapter III

Who Are Justified Through Christ

But though *He died for all,*[16] yet all do not receive the benefit of His death, but those only to whom the merit of His
passion is communicated; because as truly as men would not
be born unjust, if they were not born through propagation of
the seed of Adam, since by that propagation they contract
through him, when they are conceived, injustice as their own,
so if they were not born again in Christ, they would never be
justified, since in that new birth there is bestowed upon them,
through the merit of His passion, the grace by which they are
made just. For this benefit the Apostle exhorts us always *to
give thanks to the Father, who hath made us worthy to be
partakers of the lot of the saints in light, and hath delivered us
from the power of darkness, and hath translated us into the
kingdom of the Son of his love, in whom we have redemption
and remission of sins.*[17]

10 Gal. 4:4.
11 Gen. 49:10, 18.
12 Gal. 4:5.
13 Rom. 9:30.
14 *Ibid.,* 3:25.
15 See I John 2:2.
16 See II Cor. 5:15.
17 Col. 1:12-14.

Chapter IV

A Brief Description of the Justification of the Sinner and its Mode in the State of Grace

In which words is given a brief description of the justification of the sinner, as being a translation from that state in which man is born a child of the first Adam, to the state of grace and of the adoption of the sons of God through the second Adam, Jesus Christ, our Savior. This translation however cannot, since the promulgation of the Gospel, be effected except through the laver of regeneration or its desire, as it is written: *Unless a man be born again of water and the Holy Ghost, he cannot enter into the kingdom of God.*[18]

Chapter V

The Necessity of Preparation for Justification in Adults, and Whence it Proceeds

It is furthermore declared that in adults the beginning of that justification must proceed from the predisposing grace of God through Jesus Christ, that is, from His vocation, whereby, without any merits on their part, they are called; that they who by sin had been cut off from God, may be disposed through His quickening and helping grace to convert themselves to their own justification by freely assenting to and co-operating with that grace; so that, while God touches the heart of man through the illumination of the Holy Ghost, man himself neither does absolutely nothing while receiving that inspiration, since he can also reject it, nor yet is he able by his own free will and without the grace of God to move

[18] John 3:5.

himself to justice in His sight. Hence, when it is said in the sacred writings: *Turn ye to me, and I will turn to you,*[19] we are reminded of our liberty; and when we reply: *Convert us, O Lord, to thee, and we shall be converted,*[20] we confess that we need the grace of God.

CHAPTER VI

THE MANNER OF PREPARATION

Now, they [the adults] are disposed to that justice when, aroused and aided by divine grace, receiving *faith by hearing,*[21] they are moved freely toward God, believing to be true what has been divinely revealed and promised, especially that the sinner is justified by God *by his grace, through the redemption that is in Christ Jesus;*[22] and when, understanding themselves to be sinners, they, by turning themselves from the fear of divine justice, by which they are salutarily aroused, to consider the mercy of God, are raised to hope, trusting that God will be propitious to them for Christ's sake; and they begin to love Him as the fountain of all justice, and on that account are moved against sin by a certain hatred and detestation, that is, by that repentance that must be performed before baptism;[23] finally, when they resolve to receive baptism, to begin a new life and to keep the commandments of God. Of this disposition it is written: *He that cometh to God, must believe that he is, and is a rewarder to them that seek him;*[24] and, *Be of good faith, son, thy sins are forgiven thee;*[25] and,

19 Zach. 1:3.
20 Lam. 5:21.
21 Rom. 10:17.
22 *Ibid.,* 3:24.
23 Cf. Sess. XIV, chap. 4.
24 Heb. 11:6.
25 Matt. 9:2; Mark 2:5.

The fear of the Lord driveth out sin;[26] and, *Do penance, and be baptized every one of you in the name of Jesus Christ, for the remission of your sins, and you shall receive the gift of the Holy Ghost;*[27] and, *Going, therefore, teach ye all nations, baptizing them in the name of the Father, and of the Son, and of the Holy Ghost, teaching them to observe all things whatsoever I have commanded you;*[28] finally, *Prepare your hearts unto the Lord.*[29]

Chapter VII

In What the Justification of the Sinner Consists, and What Are its Causes

This disposition or preparation is followed by justification itself, which is not only a remission of sins but also the sanctification and renewal of the inward man through the voluntary reception of the grace and gifts whereby an unjust man becomes just and from being an enemy becomes a friend, that he may be *an heir according to hope of life everlasting.*[30] The causes of this justification are: the final cause is the glory of God and of Christ and life everlasting; the efficient cause is the merciful God who *washes and sanctifies*[31] gratuitously, signing and anointing *with the holy Spirit of promise, who is the pledge of our inheritance;*[32] the meritorious cause is His most beloved only begotten, our Lord Jesus Christ, who, *when we were enemies,*[33] *for the exceeding charity wherewith*

[26] Ecclus. 1:27.
[27] Acts 2:38.
[28] Matt. 28:19 f.
[29] See I Kings 7:3.
[30] Tit. 3:7.
[31] See I Cor. 6:11.
[32] Eph. 1:13 f.
[33] Rom. 5:10.

he loved us,[34] merited for us justification by His most holy passion on the wood of the cross and made satisfaction for us to God the Father; the instrumental cause is the sacrament of baptism, which is the sacrament-of faith,[35] without which no man was ever justified; finally, the single formal cause is the justice of God, not that by which He Himself is just, but that by which He makes us just, that, namely, with which we being endowed by Him, are *renewed in the spirit of our mind,*[36] and not only are we reputed but we are truly called and are just, receiving justice within us, each one according to his own measure, which the Holy Ghost distributes to everyone as He wills,[37] and according to each one's disposition and cooperation. For though no one can be just except he to whom the merits of the passion of our Lord Jesus Christ are communicated, yet this takes place in that justification of the sinner, when by the merit of the most holy passion, *the charity of God is poured forth by the Holy Ghost in the hearts*[38] of those who are justified and inheres in them; whence man through Jesus Christ, in whom he is ingrafted, receives in that justification, together with the remission of sins, all these infused at the same time, namely, faith, hope and charity. For faith, unless hope and charity be added to it, neither unites man perfectly with Christ nor makes him a living member of His body.[39] For which reason it is most truly said that *faith without works is dead*[40] and of no profit, and *in Christ Jesus neither circumcision availeth anything nor uncircumcision, but faith that worketh by charity.*[41] This faith, conformably to Apostolic tradition, catechumens ask of the Church before the sacrament of baptism, when they ask for the faith that

[34] Eph. 2:4.
[35] C.76, D.IV de cons.
[36] Eph. 4:23.
[37] See I Cor. 12:11.
[38] Rom. 5:5.
[39] Cf. *infra,* chap. 10.
[40] James 2:17, 20.
[41] Gal. 5:6, 6:15.

gives eternal life, which without hope and charity faith cannot give. Whence also they hear immediately the word of Christ: *If thou wilt enter into life, keep the commandments.*[42] Wherefore, when receiving true and Christian justice, they are commanded, immediately on being born again, to preserve it pure and spotless, as *the first robe*[43] given them through Christ Jesus in place of that which Adam by his disobedience lost for himself and for us, so that they may bear it before the tribunal of our Lord Jesus Christ and may have life eternal.

Chapter VIII

How the Gratuitous Justification of the Sinner by Faith is to be Understood

But when the Apostle says that man is justified by faith and freely,[44] these words are to be understood in that sense in which the uninterrupted unanimity of the Catholic Church has held and expressed them, namely, that we are therefore said to be justified by faith, because faith is the beginning of human salvation, the foundation and root of all justification, *without which it is impossible to please God*[45] and to come to the fellowship of His sons; and we are therefore said to be justified gratuitously, because none of those things that precede justification, whether faith or works, merit the grace of justification. For, *if by grace, it is not now by works, otherwise,* as the Apostle says, *grace is no more grace.*[46]

[42] Matt. 19:17.
[43] Luke 15:22.
[44] Rom. 3:24; 5:1.
[45] Heb. 11:6.
[46] Rom. 11:6.

Chapter IX

Against the Vain Confidence of Heretics

But though it is necessary to believe that sins neither are remitted nor ever have been remitted except gratuitously by divine mercy for Christ's sake, yet it must not be said that sins are forgiven or have been forgiven to anyone who boasts of his confidence and certainty of the remission of his sins,[47] resting on that alone, though among heretics and schismatics this vain and ungodly confidence may be and in our troubled times indeed is found and preached with untiring fury against the Catholic Church. Moreover, it must not be maintained, that they who are truly justified must needs, without any doubt whatever, convince themselves that they are justified, and that no one is absolved from sins and justified except he that believes with certainty that he is absolved and justified,[48] and that absolution and justification are effected by this faith alone, as if he who does not believe this, doubts the promises of God and the efficacy of the death and resurrection of Christ. For as no pious person ought to doubt the mercy of God, the merit of Christ and the virtue and efficacy of the sacraments, so each one, when he considers himself and his own weakness and indisposition, may have fear and apprehension concerning his own grace, since no one can know with the certainty of faith, which cannot be subject to error, that he has obtained the grace of God.

[47] Cf. *infra*, can. 12 and 13. [See the discussion of this controversial point in Stephen Pfürtner, *Luther and Aquinas on Salvation*, tr. Edward Quinn (New York, 1965). Ed. note.]
[48] *Infra*, can. 14.

Chapter X

The Increase of the Justification Received

Having, therefore, been thus justified and made the friends and *domestics of God*,[49] advancing *from virtue to virtue*,[50] they are *renewed*, as the Apostle says, *day by day*,[51] that is, *mortifying the members*,[52] of their flesh, and presenting them as instruments of justice unto sanctification,[53] they, through the observance of the commandments of God and of the Church, faith cooperating with good works, increase in that justice received through the grace of Christ and are further justified, as it is written: *He that is just, let him be justified still*;[54] and, *Be not afraid to be justified even to death*;[55] and again, *Do you see that by works a man is justified, and not by faith only?*[56] This increase of justice holy Church asks for when she prays: "Give unto us, O Lord, an increase of faith, hope and charity."[57]

Chapter XI

The Observance of the Commandments and the Necessity and Possibility Thereof

But no one, however much justified, should consider himself exempt from the observance of the commandments; no

[49] Eph. 2:19.
[50] Ps. 83:8.
[51] See II Cor. 4:16.
[52] Col. 3:5.
[53] Rom. 6:13, 19.
[54] Apoc. 22:11.
[55] Ecclus. 18:22.
[56] James 2:24.
[57] Thirteenth Sunday after Pentecost.

one should use that rash statement, once forbidden by the Fathers under anathema, that the observance of the commandments of God is impossible for one that is justified. For God does not command impossibilities, but by commanding admonishes thee to do what thou canst and to pray for what thou canst not, and aids thee that thou mayest be able.[58] *His commandments are not heavy,*[59] and *his yoke is sweet and burden light.*[60] For they who are the sons of God love Christ, but they who love Him, keep His commandments, as He Himself testifies;[61] which, indeed, with the divine help they can do. For though during this mortal life, men, however holy and just, fall at times into at least light and daily sins, which are also called venial, they do not on that account cease to be just, for that petition of the just, *forgive us our trespasses,*[62] is both humble and true; for which reason the just ought to feel themselves the more obliged to walk in the way of justice, for *being now freed from sin and made servants of God,*[63] they are able, *living soberly, justly and godly,*[64] to proceed onward through Jesus Christ, by whom they have access unto this grace.[65] For God does not forsake those who have been once justified by His grace, unless He be first forsaken by them. Wherefore, no one ought to flatter himself with faith alone, thinking that by faith alone he is made an heir and will obtain the inheritance, even though *he suffer* not *with Christ, that he may be also glorified with him.*[66] For even Christ Himself, as the Apostle says, *whereas he was the Son of God, he learned obedience by the things which he suffered, and being consummated, he became to all who obey him the cause of*

---

[58] St. Augustine, *De natura et gratia,* c.43 (50), PL, XLIV, 271.
[59] See I John 5:3.
[60] Matt. 11:30.
[61] John 14:23.
[62] Matt. 6:12.
[63] Rom. 6:18, 22.
[64] Tit. 2:12.
[65] Rom. 5:1 f.
[66] *Ibid.,* 8:17.

eternal salvation.[67] For which reason the same Apostle admonishes those justified, saying: *Know you not that they who run in the race, all run indeed, but one receiveth the prize? So run that you may obtain. I therefore so run, not as at an uncertainty; I so fight, not as one beating the air, but I chastise my body and bring it into subjection; lest perhaps when I have preached to others, I myself should become a castaway.*[68] So also the prince of the Apostles, Peter: *Labor the more, that by good works you may make sure your calling and election. For doing these things, you shall not sin at any time.*[69] From which it is clear that they are opposed to the orthodox teaching of religion who maintain that the just man sins, venially at least, in every good work;[70] or, what is more intolerable, that he merits eternal punishment; and they also assert that the just sin in all works, if, in order to arouse their sloth and to encourage themselves to run the race, they, in addition to this, that above all God may be glorified, have in view also the eternal reward,[71] since it is written: *I have inclined my heart to do thy justifications on account of the reward;*[72] and of Moses the Apostle says; that *he looked unto the reward.*[73]

Chapter XII

Rash Presumption of Predestination is to be Avoided

No one, moreover, so long as he lives this mortal life, ought in regard to the sacred mystery of divine predestination, so far presume as to state with absolute certainty that he is among

[67] Heb. 5:8 f.
[68] See I Cor. 9:24, 26 f.
[69] See II Pet. 1:10.
[70] Cf. *infra*, can. 25.
[71] Cf. *infra*, can. 31.
[72] Ps. 118:112.
[73] Heb. 11:26.

the number of the predestined,[74] as if it were true that the one justified either cannot sin any more, or, if he does sin, that he ought to promise himself an assured repentance. For except by special revelation, it cannot be known whom God has chosen to Himself.

Chapter XIII

The Gift of Perseverance

Similarly with regard to the gift of perseverance, of which it is written: *He that shall persevere to the end, he shall be saved,*[75] which cannot be obtained from anyone except from Him who is able to make him stand who stands,[76] that he may stand perseveringly, and to raise him who falls, let no one promise himself herein something as certain with an absolute certainty, though all ought to place and repose the firmest hope in God's help. For God, unless men themselves fail in His grace, as *he has begun a good work, so will he perfect it, working to will and to accomplish.*[77] Nevertheless, let those who think themselves to stand, take heed lest they fall,[78] and with fear and trembling work out their salvation,[79] in labors, in watchings, in almsdeeds, in prayer, in fastings and chastity. For knowing that they are born again unto the hope of glory,[80] and not as yet unto glory, they ought to fear for the combat that yet remains with the flesh, with the world and with the devil, in which they cannot be victorious unless they be with the grace of God obedient to the Apostle who says: *We are debtors, not to the flesh, to live according to the flesh; for if you live*

[74] Cf. c.17, C.XXIV, q.3.
[75] Matt. 10:22; 24:13.
[76] Rom. 14:4.
[77] Phil. 1:6; 2:13.
[78] See I Cor. 10:12.
[79] Phil. 2:12.
[80] See I Pet. 1:3.

according to the flesh, you shall die, but if by the spirit
you mortify the deeds of the flesh, you shall live.[81]

CHAPTER XIV

THE FALLEN AND THEIR RESTORATION

Those who through sin have forfeited the received grace
of justification, can again be justified when, moved by God,
they exert themselves to obtain through the sacrament of
penance the recovery, by the merits of Christ, of the grace
lost.[82] For this manner of justification is restoration for those
fallen, which the holy Fathers have aptly called a second
plank after the shipwreck of grace lost.[83] For on behalf of
those who fall into sins after baptism, Christ Jesus instituted
the sacrament of penance when He said: *Receive ye the Holy*
Ghost, whose sins you shall forgive, they are forgiven them,
and whose sins you shall retain, they are retained.[84] Hence,
it must be taught that the repentance of a Christian after his
fall is very different from that at his baptism, and that it includes not only a determination to avoid sins and a hatred of
them, or *a contrite and humble heart*,[85] but also the sacra-
mental confession of those sins, at least in desire, to be made
in its season, and sacredotal absolution, as well as satisfaction by
fasts, alms, prayers and other devout exercises of the spiritual
life, not indeed for the eternal punishment, which is, together
with the guilt, remitted either by the sacrament or by the
desire of the sacrament, but for the temporal punishment
which, as the sacred writings teach, is not always wholly remitted, as is done in baptism, to those who, ungrateful to the

[81] Rom. 8:12 f.
[82] Cf. *infra,* can. 23 and 29.
[83] C.72, D.I de poenit.
[84] John 20:22 f.
[85] Ps. 50:19.

grace of God which they have received, have grieved the Holy Ghost[86] and have not feared to *violate the temple of God.*[87] Of which repentance it is written: *Be mindful whence thou art fallen; do penance, and do the first works;*[88] and again, *The sorrow that is according to God worketh penance, steadfast unto salvation;*[89] and again, *Do penance, and bring forth fruits worthy of penance.*[90]

CHAPTER XV

BY EVERY MORTAL SIN GRACE IS LOST, BUT NOT FAITH

Against the subtle wits of some also, who *by pleasing speeches and good words seduce the hearts of the innocent,*[91] it must be maintained that the grace of justification once received is lost not only by infidelity, whereby also faith itself is lost, but also by every other mortal sin, though in this case faith is not lost; thus defending the teaching of the divine law which excludes from the kingdom of God not only unbelievers, but also the faithful [who are] *fornicators, adulterers, effeminate, liers with mankind, thieves, covetous, drunkards, railers, extortioners,*[92] and all others who commit deadly sins, from which with the help of divine grace they can refrain, and on account of which they are cut off from the grace of Christ.

[86]Eph. 4:30.
[87] See I Cor. 3:17.
[88] Apoc. 2:5.
[89] See II Cor. 7:10.
[90] Matt. 3:2; 4:17; Luke 3:8.
[91] Rom. 16:18.
[92] See I Cor. 6:9 f.; I Tim. 1:9 f.

Chapter XVI

The Fruits of Justification, That is, the Merit of Good Works, and the Nature of That Merit

Therefore, to men justified in this manner, whether they have preserved uninterruptedly the grace received or recovered it when lost, are to be pointed out the words of the Apostle: *Abound in every good work, knowing that your labor is not in vain in the Lord.*[93] *For God is not unjust, that he should forget your work, and the love which you have shown in his name;*[94] and, *Do not lose your confidence, which hath a great reward.*[95] Hence, to those who work well *unto the end*[96] and trust in God, eternal life is to be offered, both as a grace mercifully promised to the sons of God through Christ Jesus, and as a reward promised by God himself, to be faithfully given to their good works and merits.[97] For this is the crown of justice which after his fight and course the Apostle declared was laid up for him, to be rendered to him by the just judge, and not only to him, but also to all that love his coming.[98] For since Christ Jesus Himself, as the head into the members and the vine into the branches,[99] continually infuses strength into those justified, which strength always precedes, accompanies and follows their good works, and without which they could not in any manner be pleasing and meritorious before God, we must believe that nothing further is wanting to those justified to prevent them from being considered to have, by those very works which have been done in God, fully satisfied

[93] See I Cor. 15:58.
[94] Heb. 6:10.
[95] Heb. 10:35.
[96] Matt. 10:22.
[97] Rom. 6:22.
[98] See II Tim. 4:8.
[99] John 15:1 f.

the divine law according to the state of this life and to have truly merited eternal life, to be obtained in its [due] time, provided they depart [this life] in grace,[100] since Christ our Savior says: *If anyone shall drink of the water that I will give him, he shall not thirst forever; but it shall become in him a fountain of water springing up unto life everlasting.*[101] Thus, neither is our own justice established as our own from ourselves,[102] nor is the justice of God ignored or repudiated, for that justice which is called ours, because we are justified by its inherence in us, that same is [the justice] of God, because it is infused into to us by God through the merit of Christ. Nor must this be omitted, that although in the sacred writings so much is attributed to good works, that even *he that shall give a drink of cold water to one of his least ones,* Christ promises, *shall not lose his reward;*[103] and the Apostle testifies that, *That which is at present momentary and light of our tribulation, worketh for us above measure exceedingly an eternal weight of glory;*[104] nevertheless, far be it that a Christian should either trust or glory in himself and not in the Lord,[105] whose bounty toward all men is so great that He wishes the things that are His gifts to be their merits. And since *in many things we all offend,*[106] each one ought to have before his eyes not only the mercy and goodness but also the severity and judgment [of God]; neither ought anyone to judge himself, even though he be not conscious to himself of anything;[107] because the whole life of man is to be examined and judged not by the judgment of man but of God, *who will bring to light the hidden things of darkness, and will make manifest the counsels of the hearts, and then shall every man*

100 Apoc. 14:13.
101 John 4:13 f.
102 Rom. 10:3; II Cor. 3:5.
103 Matt. 10:42; Mark 9:40.
104 See II Cor. 4:17.
105 See I Cor. 1:31; II Cor. 10:17.
106 James 3:2.
107 See I Cor. 4:3 f.

have praise from God,[108] who, as it is written, *will render to every man according to his works*.[109]

After this Catholic doctrine on justification, which whosoever does not faithfully and firmly accept cannot be justified, it seemer good to the holy council to add these canons, that all may know not only what they must hold and follow, but also what to avoid and shun.

Canons Concerning Justification

Canon 1. If anyone says that man can be justified before God by his own works, whether done by his own natural powers or through the teaching of the law,[110] without divine grace through Jesus Christ, let him be anathema.

Can. 2. If anyone says that divine grace through Christ Jesus is given for this only, that man may be able more easily to live justly and to merit eternal life, as if by free will without grace he is able to do both, though with hardship and difficulty, let him be anathema.

Can. 3. If anyone says that without the predisposing inspiration of the Holy Ghost[111] and without His help, man can believe, hope, love or be repentant as he ought,[112] so that the grace of justification may be bestowed upon him, let him be anathema.

Can. 4. If anyone says that man's free will moved and aroused by God, by assenting to God's call and action, in no way cooperates toward disposing and preparing itself to obtain the grace of justification, that it cannot refuse its assent if it wishes, but that, as something inanimate, it does nothing whatever and is merely passive, let him be anathema.

108 *Ibid.*, 4:5.
109 Matt. 16:27; Rom. 2:6; Apoc. 22:12.
110 Cf. *supra*, chaps. 1, 3.
111 *Ibid.*, chap. 5.
112 Rom. 5:5.

Can. 5. If anyone says that after the sin of Adam man's free will was lost and destroyed, or that it is a thing only in name, indeed a name without a reality, a fiction introduced into the Church by Satan, let him be anathema.

Can. 6. In anyone says that it is not in man's power to make his ways evil, but that the works that are evil as well as those that are good God produces, not permissively only but also *proprie et per se*, so that the treason of Judas is no less His own proper work than the vocation of St. Paul, let him be anathema.

Can. 7. If anyone says that all works done before justification, in whatever manner they may be done, are truly sins, or merit the hatred of God; that the more earnestly one strives to dispose himself for grace, the more grievously he sins, let him be anathema.

Can. 8. If anyone says that the fear of hell,[113] whereby, by grieving for sins, we flee to the mercy of God or abstain from sinning, is a sin or makes sinners worse, let him be anathema.

Can. 9. If anyone says that the sinner is justified by faith alone,[114] meaning that nothing else is required to cooperate in order to obtain the grace of justification, and that it is not in any way necessary that he be prepared and disposed by the action of his own will, let him be anathema.

Can. 10. If anyone says that men are justified without the justice of Christ,[115] whereby He merited for us, or by that justice are formally just, let him be anathema.

Can. 11. If anyone says that men are justified either by the sole imputation of the justice of Christ or by the sole remission of sins, to the exclusion of the grace and *the charity which is poured forth in their hearts by the Holy Ghost*,[116] and remains in them, or also that the grace by which we are

[113] Matt. 10:28; Luke 12:5.
[114] *Supra,* chaps. 7, 8.
[115] Gal. 2:16; *supra,* chap. 7.
[116] Rom. 5:5.

justified is only the good will of God, let him be anathema.

Can. 12. If anyone says that justifying faith is nothing else than confidence in divine mercy,[117] which remits sins for Christ's sake, or that it is this confidence alone that justifies us, let him be anathema.

Can. 13. If anyone says that in order to obtain the remission of sins it is necessary for every man to believe with certainty and without any hesitation arising from his own weakness and indisposition that his sins are forgiven him, let him be anathema.

Can. 14. If anyone says that man is absolved from his sins and justified because he firmly believes that he is absolved and justified,[118] or that no one is truly justified except him who believes himself justified, and that by this faith alone absolution and justification are effected, let him be anathema.

Can. 15. If anyone says that a man who is born again and justified is bound *ex fide* to believe that he is certainly in the number of the predestined,[119] let him be anathema.

Can. 16. If anyone says that he will for certain, with an absolute and infallible certainty, have that great gift of perseverance even to the end, unless he shall have learned this by a special revelation,[120] let him be anathema.

Can. 17. If anyone says that the grace of justification is shared by those only who are predestined to life, but that all others who are called are called indeed but receive not grace, as if they are by divine power predestined to evil, let him be anathema.

Can. 18. If anyone says that the commandments of God are, even for one that is justified and constituted in grace,[121] impossible to observe, let him be anathema.

Can. 19. If anyone says that nothing besides faith is com-

---

[117] *Supra,* chap. 9.
[118] *Supra,* chap. 9.
[119] *Ibid.;* chap. 12.
[120] *Ibid.,* chap. 13.
[121] *Ibid.,* chap. 11.

manded in the Gospel, that other things are indifferent, neither commanded nor forbidden, but free; or that the ten commandments in no way pertain to Christians, let him be anathema.

Can. 20. If anyone says that a man who is justified and however perfect is not bound to observe the commandments of God and the Church, but only to believe,[122] as if the Gospel were a bare and absolute promise of eternal life without the condition of observing the commandments, let him be anathema.

Can. 21. If anyone says that Christ Jesus was given by God to men as a redeemer in whom to trust, and not also as a legislator whom to obey, let him be anathema.

Can. 22. If anyone says that the one justified either can without the special help of God persevere in the justice received,[123] or that with that help he cannot, let him be anathema.

Can. 23. If anyone says that a man once justified can sin no more, nor lose grace,[124] and that therefore he that falls and sins was never truly justified; or on the contrary, that he can during his whole life avoid all sins, even those that are venial, except by a special privilege from God, as the Church holds in regard to the Blessed Virgin, let him be anathema.

Can. 24. If anyone says that the justice received is not preserved and also not increased before God through good works,[125] but that those works are merely the fruits and signs of justification obtained, but not the cause of its increase, let him be anathema.

Can. 25. If anyone says that in every good work the just man sins at least venially,[126] or, what is more intolerable, mortally, and hence merits eternal punishment, and that he is

[122] Cf. chap. cit.
[123] *Supra*, chap. 13.
[124] *Ibid.*, chap. 14.
[125] *Ibid.*, chap. 10.
[126] *Ibid.*, chap. 11 at the end.

damned for this reason only, because God does not impute these works unto damnation, let him be anathema.

Can. 26. If anyone says that the just ought not for the good works done in God[127] to expect and hope for an eternal reward from God through His mercy and the merit of Jesus Christ, if by doing well and by keeping the divine commandments they persevere to the end,[128] let him be anathema.

Can. 27. If anyone says that there is no mortal sin except that of unbelief,[129] or that grace once received is not lost through any other sin however grievous and enormous except by that of unbelief, let him be anathema.

Can. 28. If anyone says that with the loss of grace through sin faith is also lost with it, or that the faith which remains is not a true faith, though it is not a living one, or that he who has faith without charity is not a Chrristian, let him be anathema.

Can. 29. If anyone says that he who has fallen after baptism cannot by the grace of God rise again,[130] or that he can indeed recover again the lost justice but by faith alone without the sacrament of penance, contrary to what the holy Roman and Universal Church, instructed by Christ the Lord and His Apostles, has hitherto professed, observed and taught, let him be anathema.

Can. 30. If anyone says that after the reception of the grace of justification the guilt is so remitted and the debt of eternal punishment so blotted out to every repentant sinner, that no debt of temporal punishment remains to be discharged either in this world[131] or in purgatory before the gates of heaven can be opened,[132] let him be anathema.

Can. 31. If anyone says that the one justified sins when he

---

[127] *Ibid.*, chap. 16.
[128] Matt. 24:13.
[129] *Supra*, chap. 15.
[130] *Ibid.*, chap. 14.
[131] Cf. Sess. XIV, chap. 8.
[132] Cf. Sess. XXV at the beginning.

performs good works with a view to an eternal reward,[133] let him be anathema.

Can. 32. If anyone says that the good works of the one justified are in such manner the gifts of God that they are not also the good merits of him justified; or that the one justified by the good works that he performs by the grace of God and the merit of Jesus Christ, whose living member he is, does not truly merit an increase of grace, eternal life, and in case he dies in grace, the attaintment of eternal life itself and also an increase of glory, let him be anathema.

Can. 33. If anyone says that the Catholic doctrine of justification as set forth by the holy council in the present decree, derogates in some respect from the glory of God or the merits of our Lord Jesus Christ, and does not rather illustrate the truth of our faith and no less the glory of God and of Christ Jesus, let him be anathema.

[133] *Supra,* chap. 11 at the end.